Simple
ITALIAN
COOKING

CHUCK WILLIAMS
COLLECTION

RECIPES BY CHUCK WILLIAMS

PHOTOGRAPHS BY ALLAN ROSENBERG

WELDON OWEN

First published in the USA in 1995 by
Weldon Owen Inc.
814 Montgomery Street
San Francisco, CA 94133

In collaboration with Williams-Sonoma
100 North Point, San Francisco, CA 94133

The Chuck Williams Collection
conceived and produced by Weldon Owen Inc.

WILLIAMS-SONOMA
Founder/Vice-Chairman: Chuck Williams

WELDON OWEN INC.
President: John Owen
Publisher/Vice-President: Wendely Harvey
Associate Publisher: Laurie Wertz
Consulting Editor: Norman Kolpas
Copy Editor: Sharon Silva
Design: John Bull, The Book Design Company
Design Layout: Janique Gascoigne
Production Director: Stephanie Sherman
Production Editor: Janique Gascoigne
Co-Editions Director: Derek Barton
Co-Editions Production Manager (US): Tarji Mickelson
Photography: Allan Rosenberg
Additional Photography: Allen V. Lott
Prop Stylist: Sandra Griswold
Food Stylist: Heidi Gintner
Assistant Food Stylist: Nette Scott
Assistant Food & Prop Stylist: Elizabeth C. Davis
Illustrations: Alice Harth

Library of Congress Cataloging-in-Publication Data:

Williams, Chuck.
    Simple Italian cooking / recipes by Chuck Williams ;
  photographs by Allan Rosenberg.
        p.   cm. — (Chuck Williams collection)
    Includes index.
    ISBN 1-875137-13-0
    1. Cookery, Italian.   I. Title.
    II. Series: Williams, Chuck.
  Chuck Williams collection
  TX723.W56   1995
  641.5945—dc20   94-32475
                                          CIP

Production by Mandarin Offset, Hong Kong
Printed in China

A Note on Weights & Measures:
All recipes include customary US, UK and
metric measurements. Conversions are
based on a standard developed for these
books and have been rounded off.
Actual weights may vary.

Contents

Introduction 5

Antipasti 6

FIRST COURSES
Soups 20
Salads 30

Pasta, Polenta
& Rice 36

SECOND COURSES
Chicken 50
Meat 60
Seafood 72
Vegetables 84

Bread 100
Desserts 106

Basic Recipes 118
Equipment 120
Suggested Menus 122
Italian Ingredients 123
Techniques 124

Acknowledgments 127
Index 127

INTRODUCTION

I made my first trip to Italy in the late 1950s. Since then, I've visited the country many times in search of the best in cookware and foods for Williams-Sonoma.

What impressed me on that first visit, and still impresses me today, was the utter simplicity of Italian cooking. Salads of garden-fresh greens lightly glistening with aromatic dressings. Pastas of all shapes tossed with quickly prepared sauces. Meats, poultry and seafood hot from the grill or stove top, fragrant with fresh herbs. Satisfying, simple desserts that leave the palate refreshed. And loaves of crusty bread that are the perfect accompaniment to every meal.

Over the past three decades or so, this straightforward Italian approach to cooking has helped change the way Americans eat. Our love of olive oil and our passion for pasta; our appreciation of such salad leaves as arugula and radicchio and of plum tomatoes; our increasing use of oregano, marjoram, sage, basil and other fresh herbs: All these trends may be traced back to the simple, delicious foods of the Italian kitchen.

I also find that the flexibility of the Italian menu and its range of ingredients suits our eating habits today, as we seek out a variety of fresh foods that are high in carbohydrates and low in fat. Enter nearly any trattoria and you're presented with a wide range of choices from which to compose a meal. Go for three or more courses, if you're so inclined. Or have just a

selection of *antipasti* and some bread. If you have a light appetite, make a meal of salad followed by soup or pasta, or even enjoy a large bowl of soup on its own. (You'll find more specific suggestions for composing menus on page 122.)

I've organized the recipes in this book to give you just such a maximum of flexibility, allowing you to pick and choose from chapters on *antipasti,* soups, salads, pastas, main courses, vegetable side dishes, breads and desserts. All of the recipes are easy to make and use readily available ingredients. They are recipes that I believe reflect the best in Italian food. The selection is entirely my own and is not meant to represent Italian cooking as a whole.

Simply put, these are my favorite Italian dishes. Along with them, I've included some useful cooking tips I've learned over the years. And you'll also find guides to kitchen equipment, cooking techniques and Italian ingredients that might come in handy as you prepare meals from this book.

All you need to round out your menu is wine, if you wish. The best advice I can give you is to find any Italian wine you like—or, for that matter, one from France, America, Australia or anywhere else—and enjoy it with your food.

Beyond that, the only thing that remains for me to say is, as one always hears in Italy, *"Buon appetito!"*

NOTES

Italy's tradition of *antipasto*—literally "before the meal"—lends itself to the way many people cook and eat today. A varied selection of easily made first-course dishes, *antipasti* can also become a satisfying meal on their own, accompanied by a hearty salad or combination of cooked vegetables. I present three dishes here that are typical of those you might find served in Italy.

Fresh baby artichokes are becoming more common in the marketplace, especially during spring and early summer. They are far superior to bottled or frozen ones. Look for young, very fresh artichokes, with small, tender leaves held tightly together.

For the mushroom salad, pick out mushrooms that feel solid and show no signs of browning of the gills concealed underneath the caps.

Choose a ripe-but-firm slicing variety of tomato. For the cheese, the best choice is fresh mozzarella, sold packed in water, but Italian Taleggio or stracchino or a soft American teleme can also be used.

ASSORTED ANTIPASTI

2–3 cups (14–21 oz/440–655 g) drained, cooked cannellini beans *(recipe on page 118)*
5 tablespoons (3 fl oz/80 ml) fresh lemon juice, plus 1 lemon, cut in half
12 tablespoons (6 fl oz/180 ml) extra-virgin olive oil
Salt and freshly ground pepper
8–10 baby artichokes, 12–16 oz (375–500 g) total weight
1 tablespoon chopped fresh mint
½ lb (250 g) small fresh mushrooms, stems trimmed and thinly sliced
20 small European black olives, such as Gaeta, Kalamata or Niçoise, drained
1 tablespoon balsamic vinegar
4–6 crisp lettuce leaves
3 ripe tomatoes, cut crosswise into slices ¼ inch (6 mm) thick
8–10 oz (250–315 g) fresh mozzarella cheese, cut into slices ¼ inch (6 mm) thick
2 tablespoons finely shredded fresh basil leaves
12–16 crostini *(recipe on page 119)*

Prepare the beans as directed. Drain and place in a bowl. While still warm, sprinkle 1 tablespoon of the lemon juice over the beans and toss. Add 3 tablespoons of the olive oil and salt and pepper to taste. Toss well; adjust the seasoning. Set aside.

❦ Fill a saucepan three-fourths full of water and squeeze in the juice from the lemon halves. Trim the artichokes (see glossary, page 126). Cut lengthwise into quarters and add at once to the lemon water to keep them from turning brown.

❦ Bring the pan of artichokes to a boil over high heat, add 2 teaspoons salt and reduce the heat to medium-low. Cook gently, uncovered, until tender, about 10 minutes. Drain well and place in a bowl. Add 2 tablespoons of the lemon juice and toss to coat evenly. Add 3 tablespoons of the olive oil, the mint, and salt and pepper to taste. Toss again and set aside to cool.

❦ Place the sliced mushrooms in a bowl. Sprinkle with the remaining 2 tablespoons lemon juice and turn gently to coat evenly. Add the olives and, while stirring carefully, drizzle with 3 tablespoons of the olive oil. Season to taste with salt and pepper and set aside.

❦ In a small bowl, combine the balsamic vinegar and salt and pepper to taste. Stir until dissolved. Whisk in the remaining 3 tablespoons olive oil. Set aside.

❦ To serve, arrange a nest of 2 or 3 lettuce leaves on one end of a large platter. Spoon the artichokes into the nest. Place the beans in the center of the platter. Arrange the tomatoes and mozzarella on top, alternating the slices. Drizzle the dressing over the tomatoes and cheese and then sprinkle with the basil. On the other end of the platter, arrange another nest of 2 or 3 lettuce leaves and top with the mushrooms. Serve immediately with crostini on the side.

SERVES 4–6

If you've ever joined the noontime crowd at a bar in the business section of an Italian city, you know what many Italians eat for lunch—bruschetta, a sandwich with a difference.

A thick slice of rustic country bread is grilled or toasted and, while still hot, rubbed with a cut piece of garlic, drizzled with fruity olive oil and topped with a wide variety of flavorful fare: grilled vegetables, soft cheeses, meats and so on. Although customers at a bar stand and eat bruschetta out of hand, at a table a knife and fork are the custom, transforming the bruschetta into a first course that can be as simple or as elegant as you wish.

For the tomato-topped bruschetta, seek out sun-ripened tomatoes and fresh young basil. The cheese bruschetta is best with an Italian-style ricotta, which has a creamier texture and better taste than most American versions; you'll find it in specialty-food stores or high-quality markets. Be sure to locate flat-leaf parsley, too, which has a more pronounced flavor than the crinkly-leafed variety.

BRUSCHETTA TRIO

1 red bell pepper (capsicum)
1 yellow bell pepper (capsicum)
2 tablespoons extra-virgin olive oil, plus extra for drizzling
2 cloves garlic, minced, plus 2 cloves garlic, cut in half
Salt and freshly ground pepper
4 ripe plum (Roma) tomatoes
1 tender celery stalk, cut into small dice (½ cup/2½ oz/75 g)
3 green (spring) onions, including some tender green tops, chopped
2 tablespoons chopped fresh basil
1 cup (8 oz/250 g) ricotta cheese, preferably Italian style, drained of any liquid
½ cup (¾ oz/20 g) coarsely chopped flat-leaf (Italian) parsley
1 teaspoon fresh lemon juice, plus 1 lemon
12 slices crusty country-style Italian or French bread, each about ½ inch (12 mm) thick and 3½–4 inches (9–10 cm) in diameter

Roast and peel the bell peppers (see glossary, page 125). Cut the peppers lengthwise into strips ¼ inch (6 mm) wide. Set aside.

❧ In a saucepan over medium-low heat, warm the 2 tablespoons olive oil. Add the 2 minced garlic cloves and sauté gently, stirring, for 30–40 seconds. Add the bell peppers and sauté until just tender, 5–6 minutes. Season to taste with salt and pepper, transfer to a bowl and cover to keep warm.

❧ Core the tomatoes and cut in half crosswise. Gently squeeze out the seeds. Cut into small dice and place in a separate bowl. Add the celery, green onions and basil, and season to taste with salt and pepper. Stir to blend. Set aside at room temperature.

❧ In another bowl, combine the ricotta cheese, parsley and the 1 teaspoon lemon juice. Stir to mix well and season to taste with salt and pepper. Set aside at room temperature.

❧ When ready to serve, preheat a broiler (griller). Place the bread slices on a baking sheet and place under the broiler. Toast, turning once, until lightly golden, about 1½ minutes on each side. Remove the bread from the broiler and immediately rub 1 side of each slice with the cut side of a garlic clove. Drizzle or brush the garlic-rubbed sides evenly and lightly with olive oil.

❧ To serve, top 4 of the warm bread slices with the bell pepper slices. Top 4 of the slices with the tomato mixture. Top the final 4 slices with the ricotta cheese mixture. Using a zester or small shredder (see glossary, page 126), shred the zest (yellow part only) from the skin of the lemon directly over the bruschetta topped with the ricotta mixture. Place on plates and serve immediately.

SERVES 4–6

SHRIMP-FILLED ARTICHOKES WITH MUSTARD DRESSING

1 lemon, plus 2 tablespoons fresh lemon juice
4 large but young artichokes
2 tablespoons coriander seeds
2 bay leaves
Salt
1 lb (500 g) small shrimp (prawns), peeled (leave tail fin attached) and deveined
2 teaspoons Dijon mustard
2 tablespoons chopped fresh basil
⅔ cup (5 fl oz/160 ml) extra-virgin olive oil
Freshly ground pepper

Cut the lemon in half and squeeze the juice into a bowl. Trim the artichokes (see glossary, page 126). As each one is trimmed, brush the cut surfaces with the lemon juice. Spread open the center and, using a small spoon, scoop out the choke (thistlelike core).

🐚 Make a bouquet garni: Place the coriander seeds and 1 of the bay leaves in the center of a 6-inch (15-cm) square of cheesecloth (muslin). Gather together the edges, forming a sachet, and tie with kitchen string.

🐚 Fill a large saucepan three-fourths full of water and bring to a rapid boil. Add the bouquet garni, 2 teaspoons salt and any lemon juice remaining in the bowl. Add the artichokes, stem end down, allowing them to float. Reduce the heat slightly, cover partially and boil until the stem end is tender when pierced with a sharp knife, about 20 minutes. Using tongs, transfer the artichokes upside down (stem end up) to a plate. Discard the pan contents and place a double layer of paper towels on the bottom. Place the artichokes on the towels, stem end up, cover partially and set aside to cool.

🐚 Fill a small saucepan one-half full of water and bring to a boil. Add 1 teaspoon salt and the remaining bay leaf. Reduce the heat to medium-low and simmer for 5 minutes. Add the shrimp, reduce the heat to low, cover and gently poach until pink and opaque, about 2 minutes. Drain and set aside to cool slightly.

🐚 In a large bowl, make a dressing by combining the 2 tablespoons lemon juice, ⅛ teaspoon salt and the mustard, stirring until the salt dissolves. Add the basil, olive oil and pepper to taste. Whisk until well blended; taste and adjust seasoning. Add the shrimp and toss to coat well.

🐚 Transfer the artichokes to a serving platter, stem ends down. Spread open the centers. Using a slotted spoon, transfer the shrimp to the centers, dividing them equally. Pour the dressing into 4 individual bowls and serve alongside for dipping the artichoke leaves. Serve the artichokes warm or at room temperature.

SERVES 4

Large artichokes make excellent edible containers for fillings. But first their tough outer leaves must be removed, the tough upper part cut off, and the prickly choke scooped out (see page 126).

It is important to coat the cut surfaces of the artichoke with lemon juice so they do not turn brown. Cook the artichokes just until they are tender; any longer and they will be soft and soggy. Drain them well, bottoms up, on paper towels inside the still-hot pot in which they were cooked (you'll rid them of more liquid this way). For the best flavor, do not refrigerate the artichokes before serving.

Look for large but young artichokes with closely fitting leaves that look green and fresh. Too many artichokes are harvested past their prime and tend to be tough and fibrous.

GRILLED VEGETABLES WITH HERBED DRESSING

NOTES

I can think of nothing that so perfectly fits the present trend toward low-fat, low-calorie cooking as grilled vegetables. Almost all vegetables cook well and easily on the grill. They require only a light brushing of oil to lubricate them for browning, and a sprinkling of fresh herbs for extra flavor and aroma.

You can grill vegetables in one of several ways. A broiler (griller) or a charcoal grill will work beautifully. Italians most often use a stove-top grill—a cast-iron, ridged pan that provides intense, searing heat and makes the characteristic grill marks; they are available in specialty cookware stores (see page 121). If you use a stove-top grill, avoid overly juicy vegetables or too much oil, either of which can smoke up your kitchen. Slices of eggplant, zucchini, radicchio and fennel bulb cook well on a stove-top grill.

Focaccia *(optional; recipe on page 118)*
1 tablespoon fresh lemon juice
⅛ teaspoon salt
⅓ cup (3 fl oz/80 ml) extra-virgin olive oil, plus extra for brushing
1 or 2 green (spring) onions, including some tender green tops, minced
1 tablespoon chopped fresh mint, oregano, basil, flat-leaf (Italian) parsley or other herb
Freshly ground pepper
2 or 3 small Asian (slender) eggplants (aubergines), or 1 small globe eggplant
2 or 3 small zucchini (courgettes)
1 medium-sized head radicchio
2 small fennel bulbs

If using the focaccia, bake the bread as directed.

❧ In a small bowl, make a dressing by combining the lemon juice and salt, stirring until the salt dissolves. Add the ⅓ cup (3 fl oz/80 ml) olive oil, the green onions, mint or other herb, and pepper to taste. Whisk until blended; set aside.

❧ If using Asian eggplants, trim and cut lengthwise into slices ¼ inch (6 mm) thick. If using a globe eggplant, trim, cut in half lengthwise and cut each half crosswise into slices ¼ inch (6 mm) thick; then sprinkle both sides of the slices with salt, place in a single layer in a colander and let stand over a bowl or in the sink for 45 minutes to drain the bitter juices. Rinse the slices and pat dry with paper towels, pressing down to absorb all the moisture. Set aside.

❧ Preheat a broiler (griller), or prepare a fire in a charcoal grill. If using a cast-iron or cast-aluminum stove-top grill, preheat for a minute or two over medium-high heat just before putting the vegetables on.

❧ Trim the zucchini and cut lengthwise into slices ¼ inch (6 mm) thick. Discard any old leaves from the radicchio. Cut into 8 wedges. Trim the stems from the fennel bulbs; cut the bulbs lengthwise into slices ⅛ inch (3 mm) thick.

❧ Brush the vegetables lightly on both sides with olive oil. Place on the stove-top grill pan, on a broiler pan or on the rack of a charcoal grill. Grill or broil, turning once, until lightly browned and tender when pierced with the point of a knife, 4–5 minutes on each side.

❧ Whisk the dressing again and spoon a little on the bottom of a serving platter. Arrange the vegetables on the platter and spoon a little dressing over the top. Serve warm or at room temperature with the focaccia, if using. Pass any remaining dressing at the table.

SERVES 4

ASPARAGUS WITH CAPERS AND PINE NUTS

¼ cup (1½ oz/45 g) pine nuts
1½ lb (750 g) asparagus, preferably small to medium-sized spears,
  6–7 inches (15–18 cm) long
Salt
6 tablespoons (3 oz/90 g) unsalted butter
1 tablespoon fresh lemon juice
¼ cup (2 oz/60 g) drained capers
Freshly ground pepper
¼-lb (125-g) piece Italian Parmesan cheese, preferably Parmigiano-Reggiano

In a heavy frying pan over medium heat, toast the pine nuts, stirring, until lightly colored and fragrant, 1–2 minutes. Transfer to a bowl; set aside.

❧ Break or cut off any tough white ends of the asparagus spears and discard. Cut all the spears the same length. If medium-sized or larger, peel the asparagus spears as well: using a vegetable peeler or asparagus peeler and starting about 2 inches (5 cm) below the tip, peel off the outer skin from each spear.

❧ In a large sauté pan or deep frying pan that will accommodate the asparagus comfortably lying flat, add water to a depth of 2–3 inches (5–7.5 cm). Bring to a rapid boil over high heat. Add 2 teaspoons salt and the asparagus. When the water returns to a boil, reduce the heat slightly and boil gently, uncovered, until tender when pierced with a sharp knife, 4–7 minutes, depending upon their size.

❧ Meanwhile, in a small saucepan over medium-low heat, melt the butter. Add the lemon juice and capers, season to taste with pepper and cook, stirring gently, for 30–40 seconds. Taste and adjust the seasoning, adding salt, pepper or lemon juice as needed.

❧ When the asparagus spears are done, drain well and place on a serving platter or individual plates. Spoon the caper sauce over them and then scatter on the pine nuts. Using a vegetable peeler and holding the piece of Parmesan over the asparagus, shave off paper-thin slices; be generous with the cheese. Serve at once.

SERVES 4

NOTES

This first course or side dish is best served immediately after cooking, when the heat of the vegetable combines with the other ingredients to produce a lovely fragrance. Small to medium-sized asparagus spears will have the finest flavor and texture. If you purchase medium-sized or larger stalks, use a vegetable peeler or asparagus peeler (see page 121) to strip away any thick, coarse skin.

Some capers can be exceptionally salty, so drain off the brine and taste one. If they are too salty, rinse well in cold water and drain again.

If you'd prefer the asparagus spears cold, try serving them with an oil and lemon juice dressing in place of the lemon-caper sauce: Immediately after draining the asparagus stalks, plunge them into cold water to stop the cooking, then drain again. Stir together 2 tablespoons fresh lemon juice and salt and pepper to taste; then stir in ¼ cup (2 fl oz/60 ml) extra-virgin olive oil and 1 teaspoon chopped fresh tarragon. Drizzle over the asparagus and serve at room temperature.

Green Beans and Tuna with Basil

A great combination of flavors, this dish has probably been a part of the *antipasto* table for more than a century. It makes an excellent first course, a luncheon main course, or a light supper when served with a soup and a fruit dessert.

Seek out young, small green beans and cook only until tender-crisp. Red bell pepper adds a pleasant touch of color and flavor.

For the dressing, I've used fresh lemon juice instead of vinegar because it goes better with the tuna and gives the whole dish a nice freshness. I've also found that the flavors are distributed better by tossing the beans with the lemon juice before adding the oil. The dish will be at its best if assembled at the last minute and served at room temperature.

1 lb (500 g) young, tender green beans, trimmed and cut into 3–4-inch (7.5–10-cm) lengths
1 small red bell pepper (capsicum), cut in half lengthwise, seeded and deribbed
Salt
⅓ cup (2 oz/60 g) diced sweet red (Spanish) onion
2 tablespoons finely chopped fresh basil leaves
1 tablespoon fresh lemon juice, plus extra to taste
Freshly ground pepper
3 tablespoons extra-virgin olive oil, plus extra to taste
1 can (6½ oz/200 g) solid-pack tuna in olive oil, preferably imported Italian, drained
1–2 tablespoons capers (depending upon your taste), rinsed and well drained

Fill a large saucepan three-fourths full of water and bring to a rapid boil over high heat. Add the green beans, bell pepper halves and 2 teaspoons salt. Quickly bring back to a boil and cook, uncovered, until the beans are just tender but still firm, 4–5 minutes. Drain well.

Place the beans in a large bowl. Cut the pepper halves lengthwise into strips ½ inch (12 mm) wide. Add to the beans, along with the red onion and 1 tablespoon of the basil. Sprinkle with the 1 tablespoon lemon juice and a little salt and pepper to taste. Toss to coat the beans well with the lemon juice. Drizzle with the 3 tablespoons olive oil and toss again.

In a separate bowl, break the tuna into small chunks. Add the capers and the remaining 1 tablespoon basil. Season to taste with lemon juice, olive oil, pepper and a little salt, if needed. Toss gently to blend.

Arrange the beans on a serving platter or individual plates and mound the tuna mixture in the center. Serve at once.

SERVES 4

SHRIMP AND SCALLOPS WITH MIXED HERBS AND BABY GREENS

1 cup (1 oz/30 g) flat-leaf (Italian) parsley leaves, stems removed, plus
   2 tablespoons coarsely chopped parsley
1 cup (1 oz/30 g) small spinach leaves, carefully washed, stems removed
   and leaves torn into small pieces
1 cup (1 oz/30 g) small watercress sprigs, carefully washed and trimmed
½ cup (½ oz/15 g) fresh basil leaves, torn into small pieces
¼ cup fresh cilantro (fresh coriander) leaves, stems removed
¼ cup fresh dill sprigs, feathery tops only, stems removed
2 tablespoons fresh lemon juice
Salt
Dash of cayenne pepper
½ cup (4 fl oz/125 ml) extra-virgin olive oil
1 clove garlic, minced
1 green (spring) onion, including some tender green tops, minced
1 bay leaf
¾ lb (375 g) sea scallops, cut into 1-inch (2.5-cm) pieces, or bay scallops, left whole
1 lb (500 g) small or medium-sized shrimp (prawns), peeled (leave tail fin
   attached) and deveined
12–16 crostini *(recipe on page 119)*

In a bowl, toss together the 1 cup (1 oz/30 g) parsley leaves, the spinach, watercress, basil, cilantro and dill. Cover and set aside.

In another bowl, make a dressing by combining the lemon juice, ⅛ teaspoon salt and the cayenne pepper. Stir until the salt dissolves. Add the olive oil and whisk until blended. Stir in the garlic and green onion. Set aside.

Fill a saucepan one-half full of water, add 1 teaspoon salt and the bay leaf and bring to a boil over medium heat. Reduce the heat to medium-low and simmer for 5 minutes. Add the scallops, reduce the heat to low, cover and gently poach until opaque, about 2 minutes. Using a slotted spoon, transfer the scallops to a colander to drain. Raise the heat to medium-low so the water simmers steadily and add the shrimp. Again reduce the heat to low, cover and poach until pink and opaque, about 2 minutes. Using a slotted spoon, transfer the shrimp to the colander to drain completely. Then place the scallops and shrimp in a bowl, drizzle on half of the dressing and toss until well coated. Let cool.

Drizzle the remaining dressing over the greens and toss to coat. Arrange the greens around the perimeter of a serving platter. Spoon the scallops and shrimp in the center and sprinkle with the chopped parsley. Serve immediately with the warm crostini.

SERVES 4

NOTES

Since Roman times, Italians have used their native herbs in intriguing combinations with other local ingredients, and this recipe is a perfect example of that tradition. Using some of the larger-leaved herbs whole gives the dish a delightful extra dimension of flavor; you may want to try incorporating these herbs into your green salads as well.

The shrimp and scallops in this recipe are poached. If you prefer, grill or sauté them. For the grill, brush them first with olive oil. If sautéing them, heat 1 tablespoon each unsalted butter and olive oil in a sauté pan, then add the shellfish. Toss and turn until the shrimp are pink and the scallops are opaque, 2–3 minutes.

FRESH TOMATO AND BREAD SOUP WITH BASIL

3 lb (1.5 kg) ripe plum (Roma) tomatoes
3 tablespoons olive oil, plus extra for brushing on bread
1 yellow onion, chopped (1 cup/4 oz/125 g)
3 cloves garlic, minced
¼ cup firmly packed, finely shredded fresh basil leaves
¼ teaspoon sugar
Pinch of red pepper flakes
Salt and freshly ground pepper
¼ cup (2 oz/60 g) Italian Arborio rice or medium-grain white rice
6–7 cups (48–56 fl oz/1.5–1.75 l) chicken broth, heated
4 slices crusty country-style Italian or French bread, each about ½ inch
   (12 mm) thick and 3½–4 inches (9–10 cm) in diameter

Core and peel the tomatoes (see glossary, page 124). Cut the tomatoes in half crosswise and carefully squeeze out the seeds. Chop the tomatoes; you should have about 6 cups (2¼ lb/1.1 kg).

In a large saucepan over medium-low heat, warm the 3 tablespoons olive oil. Add the onion and garlic and sauté gently, stirring, until translucent, 6–7 minutes. Add the tomatoes, half of the basil leaves, the sugar, red pepper flakes, and salt and pepper to taste. Stir in the rice, cover partially; simmer until the tomatoes start to break down, 8–10 minutes. Add 6 cups (48 fl oz/1.5 l) of the chicken broth, re-cover partially and simmer until the rice is almost tender, 10–15 minutes longer.

Remove one-third of the soup from the pan. Fit a food mill with the fine disk and rest it over a bowl. Ladle the removed soup into the mill and turn the handle to purée. Alternatively, purée in a food processor with the metal blade or in a blender. Return the purée to the pot, stir well, cover partially and continue to barely simmer over low heat, stirring occasionally to prevent sticking, until the rice is tender, another 8–10 minutes. Add the remaining 1 cup (8 fl oz/250 ml) chicken broth if the soup seems too thick. Taste and adjust the seasoning.

Meanwhile, preheat an oven to 325°F (165°C). Brush each bread slice on one side with olive oil and arrange on a baking sheet, oiled side up. Place in the oven until the bread is warm, a few minutes.

To serve, place a warm bread slice in each of 4 large, warmed shallow soup bowls. Ladle the hot soup over the bread. Garnish with the remaining shredded basil and serve at once.

SERVES 4

MINESTRONE

¾ cup (5 oz/155 g) dried cannellini beans
2 cups (16 fl oz/500 ml) hot tap water
1½ lb (750 g) ripe plum (Roma) tomatoes
2 tablespoons unsalted butter
1 large yellow onion, cut into ½-inch (12-mm) dice (about 1½ cups/6 oz/185 g)
2 carrots, peeled and cut into ½-inch (12-mm) dice (about 1 cup/5 oz/155 g)
2 celery stalks, cut into ½-inch (12-mm) dice (about 1 cup/5 oz/155 g)
3 or 4 small potatoes, preferably yellow-fleshed such as Finnish Yellow or
   Alaska (Yukon) Gold, or russet, peeled and cut into ¾-inch (2-cm) dice
2 or 3 fresh oregano sprigs
6 cups (48 fl oz/1.5 l) chicken broth
4 or 5 green Swiss chard leaves, carefully washed, stems removed, and leaves cut
   into strips ¼ inch (6 mm) wide (about 1½ cups/2 oz/60 g firmly packed)
1 cup (3½ oz/105 g) elbow macaroni or other short dried pasta
Salt and freshly ground pepper
8–10 fresh basil leaves, cut into fine shreds
1 cup (4 oz/125 g) freshly grated Italian Parmesan cheese, preferably
   Parmigiano-Reggiano

Sort through the beans, discarding any discolored ones or impurities. Rinse the beans, drain and place in a saucepan with hot tap water to cover by 2 inches (5 cm). Place over medium-high heat and bring to a boil. Immediately remove from the heat, cover and let stand for 1 hour. Drain, rinse and drain again. Return the beans to the pan and add the 2 cups (16 fl oz/500 ml) hot tap water. Place over medium-high heat and bring to a simmer. Reduce the heat to medium-low, cover and simmer until the beans are tender, 1–1½ hours. Set aside.

While the beans are cooking, core and peel the tomatoes (see glossary, page 124). Cut the tomatoes in half crosswise and carefully squeeze out the seeds. Chop the tomatoes; you should have 2½–3 cups (15–18 oz/470–560 g). Set aside.

In a large saucepan over medium-low heat, melt the butter. Add the onion and sauté until translucent, 6–7 minutes. Add the carrots and celery and sauté until beginning to soften, 4–5 minutes. Add the potatoes, tomatoes, oregano and broth, raise the heat and bring to a simmer. Reduce the heat to medium-low, cover and simmer until the potatoes are almost tender, about 20 minutes.

Add the chard and the cannellini beans and their liquid and stir well. Cover and simmer over medium-low heat until the chard is tender, about 15 minutes longer. Add the pasta, cover and simmer until the pasta is tender, about 15 minutes longer. Season to taste with salt and pepper.

To serve, ladle into warmed bowls. Sprinkle with the basil and cheese.

SERVES 4–6

Every region of Italy has its own version of this hearty vegetable soup, and as you travel the country you find that the choice of vegetables varies along with the inclusion of pasta, dried beans or rice—alone or in pairs. I've included macaroni and cannellini beans. I recommend cannellini beans because they have good flavor and texture. You can, however, substitute Great Northern or small white lima beans. And if fresh oregano is not available, use ½ teaspoon dried.

For the soup to be at its best, the vegetables must be cooked in the prescribed sequence, so that the longer-cooking vegetables go in first. Once the pasta has been added, the soup should continue cooking only until the pasta is *al dente* (tender but still chewy).

Have good Italian Parmesan cheese on hand to sprinkle on top. Serve crusty country-style bread alongside.

LENTIL, TOMATO AND MINT SOUP

NOTES

I first encountered this soup of lentils and tomatoes flavored with fresh mint years ago in Rome. I was intrigued with its unexpectedly delicious combination of tastes, which probably shows the influence of North African cooking from the days of the Roman Empire. The mint contributes a marvelously light, refreshing flavor; do not substitute dried mint, which simply cannot compare.

The soup is so satisfying that all you need is good crusty bread and a green salad to make a splendid lunch.

2 cups (14 oz/440 g) dried lentils
6 cups (48 fl oz/1.5 l) water
Salt
3 lb (1.5 kg) ripe plum (Roma) tomatoes
3 tablespoons olive oil
2 medium-sized yellow onions, chopped (2–2½ cups/8–10 oz/250–315 g)
¼ cup chopped fresh mint, plus extra for garnish
4 cups (32 fl oz/1 l) chicken broth, or as needed
Freshly ground pepper

Sort through the lentils, discarding any discolored ones or impurities. Rinse the lentils, drain and place in a large saucepan with the water. Place over medium-high heat, add 2 teaspoons salt and bring just to a boil. Reduce the heat to medium-low, cover partially and simmer until the lentils are tender, about 30 minutes. Drain and set aside.

While the lentils are cooking, core and peel the tomatoes (see glossary, page 124). Cut the tomatoes in half crosswise and carefully squeeze out the seeds. Chop the tomatoes coarsely; you should have 5½–6 cups (33–36 oz/530–625 g). Set aside.

In a large saucepan over medium-low heat, warm the olive oil. Add the onions and sauté gently, stirring, until translucent, 6–7 minutes. Add the tomatoes and the ¼ cup mint and cook gently, uncovered, until the tomatoes break down and the juices are released, 10–15 minutes longer.

Stir in the chicken broth and the reserved lentils, cover partially and barely simmer over medium-low heat until the flavors are well blended and everything is tender, 10–15 minutes longer. Add more chicken broth or water if the soup seems too thick. Season to taste with salt and pepper.

To serve, ladle into warmed bowls and sprinkle with chopped mint.

SERVES 4–6

SPINACH AND RICE SOUP

½ cup (3½ oz/105 g) dried chick-peas (garbanzo beans)
6 cups (48 fl oz/1.5 l) chicken broth
1 cup (8 fl oz/250 ml) dry white wine or water
2 bunches spinach, 1½–2 lb (750 g–1 kg) total weight
¼ cup (2 fl oz/60 ml) water
1 tablespoon olive oil
1 small yellow onion, finely chopped (about ½ cup/2 oz/60 g)
1 clove garlic, finely chopped (about 1 teaspoon)
½ cup (3½ oz/105 g) Italian Arborio rice or medium-grain white rice
Salt and freshly ground pepper
Freshly grated nutmeg

Sort through the chick-peas, discarding any discolored ones or impurities. Rinse the chick-peas, drain and place in a bowl. Add hot tap water to cover by 2 inches (5 cm) and let soak for 1 hour. Drain, rinse again and place in a saucepan with hot tap water to cover by 1 inch (2.5 cm). Place over medium-high heat and bring to a boil. Reduce the heat to medium-low, cover and simmer until tender, about 1 hour. Drain and set aside.

In a saucepan over medium heat, combine the chicken broth and the 1 cup (8 fl oz/250 ml) wine or water. Heat to just under a boil. Reduce the heat to low and keep warm.

Pick over the spinach, discarding any old or damaged leaves, and wash well. Remove the stems. Gather the leaves together in bundles and chop coarsely. Place in a large sauté pan or saucepan and add the ¼ cup (2 fl oz/60 ml) water. Cover, place over medium heat and cook, stirring a couple of times to cook evenly, until the spinach wilts, 1–2 minutes. Transfer to a colander and, using a kitchen spoon, press against the spinach to remove all the liquid. Set aside.

In a large pot or saucepan over medium-low heat, warm the olive oil. Add the onion and garlic and sauté gently, stirring, until translucent, 4–5 minutes. Add the rice and stir until the rice is coated with the oil, 2–3 minutes.

Stirring constantly, slowly pour in the hot broth mixture. Then add the spinach and chick-peas and bring to a simmer. Cover partially and simmer gently over low heat, stirring occasionally, until the rice is cooked just to the *al dente* stage (tender but firm to the bite), 20–25 minutes. Season to taste with salt and pepper and a little nutmeg. If the soup is too thick, add a little water to achieve the proper consistency.

To serve, ladle into warmed bowls and serve immediately.

SERVES 4

CANNELLINI BEAN SOUP

NOTES

5 cups (2¼ lb/1.1 kg) drained, cooked cannellini beans *(recipe on page 118)*
1 red bell pepper (capsicum)
3 tablespoons olive oil
3 cloves garlic, chopped
1 yellow onion, diced (1 cup/4 oz/125 g)
1 carrot, peeled and diced (½ cup/2½ oz/75 g)
1 celery stalk, diced (½ cup/2½ oz/75 g)
2 teaspoons chopped fresh oregano
6 cups (48 fl oz/1.5 l) chicken broth
Salt and freshly ground pepper
1 cup (3½ oz/105 g) dried spinach fusilli (spiral) pasta
½ cup (2 oz/60 g) freshly grated romano cheese

This simple white bean soup is one of Italy's finest, and the addition of pasta makes it especially satisfying. I cook the pasta separately and then add it at serving time to ensure the pasta is cooked properly—neither underdone nor overcooked.

If you can't find Italian cannellini beans—usually sold in Italian markets or specialty-food stores—use Great Northern beans instead. Search out good Italian romano cheese, too. If fresh oregano is unavailable, substitute 1 teaspoon dried.

Cook the beans as directed. Drain and set aside.

Roast and peel the bell pepper (see glossary, page 125). Cut lengthwise into strips ½ inch (12 mm) wide, then cut the strips in half crosswise. Set aside.

In a large, deep saucepan over medium-low heat, warm 2 tablespoons of the olive oil. Add the garlic and sauté, stirring, for 30–40 seconds. Add the onion and sauté gently, stirring, until translucent, 4–5 minutes. Add the carrot, celery and oregano and sauté, stirring, until they begin to soften, 4–5 minutes.

Raise the heat to medium-high and add the reserved beans, the bell pepper and chicken broth. Bring to a simmer, reduce the heat to medium-low, cover and simmer until the vegetables are tender, about 20 minutes. Season to taste with salt and pepper.

Remove 3 cups (24 fl oz/750 ml) of the soup from the pan. Fit a food mill with the fine disk and rest it over a bowl. Ladle the removed soup into the mill and turn the handle to purée. Alternatively, purée in a food processor fitted with the metal blade or in a blender. Return the purée to the pot, stir well and simmer over low heat for 4–5 minutes to blend the textures. Watch carefully that the bean purée does not scorch.

Fill a saucepan three-fourths full of water and bring to a boil over medium-high heat. Add the pasta, 2 teaspoons salt and the remaining 1 tablespoon olive oil. Cook until the pasta is *al dente* (tender but still firm to the bite), 5–6 minutes, or according to the package instructions. Drain and keep warm.

To serve, ladle the soup into warmed bowls and add cooked pasta to each bowl. Sprinkle with the romano cheese and serve at once.

SERVES 4–6

Escarole Salad with Pear and Prosciutto

NOTES

Here is a salad that you might find served by the shore at Portofino in late summer. It makes an excellent first course, either for a dinner party or a weekend lunch.

If escarole is unavailable, substitute chicory (curly endive), oak-leaf lettuce or some other flavorful lettuce variety. If you cannot find fresh tarragon, use fresh mint. Be generous with the tarragon or mint, as they are both mild flavors.

Comice pears are large, round fruits with short necks and greenish yellow skins blushed with red. They are sweet and juicy, and I find they are the best choice to serve with prosciutto. You could, however, substitute Red Bartlett, d'Anjou or Royal Riviera pears.

1 large head escarole
3 or 4 fresh tarragon sprigs
1 tablespoon fresh lemon juice, plus juice of 1 lemon
⅛ teaspoon salt
1 teaspoon Dijon mustard
Freshly ground pepper
¼ cup (2 fl oz/60 ml) extra-virgin olive oil
2 ripe but firm pears, preferably Comice *(see note)*
16 thin, lean prosciutto slices
¾ cup (4½ oz/140 g) ripe red seedless grapes, stems removed

Separate the leaves from the head of escarole, discarding any old or damaged leaves. Wash carefully, dry well and tear into large bite-sized pieces. Place in a bowl. Remove the leaves from the tarragon sprigs and tear or chop into small pieces. Add to the bowl with the escarole and toss to mix. Cover with a damp towel and refrigerate to crisp.

In a small bowl, combine the 1 tablespoon lemon juice and the salt. Stir to dissolve the salt. Stir in the mustard and pepper to taste. Add the olive oil and whisk until well blended. Taste and adjust the seasoning. Set aside.

Place the juice of 1 lemon in a large bowl. Cut the pears into quarters, remove the stems and cores, and then cut each quarter into 2 wedges. Place the pear wedges in the bowl with the lemon juice and toss carefully to coat all cut surfaces (this prevents them from darkening).

Carefully separate the prosciutto slices and then wrap a slice around each pear wedge.

Whisk the dressing again and pour it over the greens. Toss to mix well. Divide the greens among 4 salad plates. Scatter the grapes over the greens (if the grapes are large, you may want to cut them in half). Arrange 4 prosciutto-wrapped pear wedges on each plate, next to the salad. Serve at once.

SERVES 4

BLOOD ORANGE, FENNEL AND OLIVE SALAD

Quickly becoming a classic in Italy's more sophisticated restaurants, this salad is fresh tasting, light and low in fat—three requisites for healthful eating. Blood oranges are the first choice, but you can use regular oranges as well. Fresh fennel is available almost everywhere now; look for smaller bulbs, which are more tender. And do use Italian or Greek black olives, or even French Niçoise olives. Cured in brine, these flavorful olives are all now widely distributed in the United States.

Although balsamic vinegar is becoming popular now, beware of large bottles at cheap prices, which offer little more than a lightly flavored wine vinegar. True balsamic vinegar, which is aged for many years, should have a mildly tart-sweet flavor and a rich, dark color.

1 head chicory (curly endive)
4 or 5 fresh cilantro (fresh coriander) sprigs
2 small fennel bulbs, 1–1½ lb (500–750 g) total weight
4 or 5 blood oranges, preferably seedless, 1½–2 lb (750 g–1 kg) total weight
2 tablespoons balsamic vinegar
⅛ teaspoon salt
⅓ cup (3 fl oz/80 ml) extra-virgin olive oil
1 teaspoon honey
1–2 teaspoons fresh orange juice
Freshly ground pepper
16–20 small European black olives, such as Gaeta, Kalamata or Niçoise

Separate the leaves from the head of chicory, discarding any old or damaged leaves. Wash carefully, dry well and tear into bite-sized pieces. Place in a bowl. Remove the leaves from the cilantro sprigs and tear or chop into small pieces. Add to the bowl with the chicory and toss to mix. Cover with a damp towel and refrigerate to crisp.

 Trim off any stems and bruised stalks from the fennel bulbs. Cut crosswise into paper-thin slices. Place in a separate bowl and set aside.

 Cut a thick slice off the top and bottom of each orange, exposing the fruit beneath the peel. Working with 1 orange at a time, place upright on a cutting surface and, holding the orange firmly, thickly slice off the peel in wide strips, cutting off the pith and membrane with it to reveal the fruit sections. Cut the oranges crosswise into slices ¼ inch (6 mm) thick. Remove any seeds and discard. Place the orange slices in yet another bowl and set aside.

 In a small bowl, combine the balsamic vinegar and salt. Stir to dissolve the salt. Add the olive oil, honey and orange juice and whisk until well blended. Add pepper to taste. Taste and adjust the seasoning.

 To serve, whisk the dressing again and drizzle half of it over the fennel. Toss to coat well. Arrange the fennel in a mound in the center of a platter or individual plates. Arrange the chicory around the fennel, then arrange the orange slices over the chicory. Drizzle the remaining dressing over the orange slices and chicory. Scatter the olives over the top. Serve immediately.

SERVES 4

ARUGULA SALAD WITH BLACK OLIVE CROSTINI

2 tablespoons capers, drained and chopped
2 cloves garlic, chopped (1 teaspoon)
1 teaspoon chopped fresh oregano
1 tablespoon drained, boned and mashed sardines
4 tablespoons extra-virgin olive oil
1 cup (5 oz/155 g) drained, pitted European black olives,
   such as Gaeta, Kalamata or Spanish, chopped
1 lemon
12–16 crostini *(recipe on page 119)*
1–2 bunches arugula (rocket), 8–9 oz (250–280 g) total weight
1 tablespoon white wine vinegar
⅛ teaspoon salt
1 tablespoon walnut oil *(see note)*
Freshly ground pepper

In a food processor fitted with the metal blade or in a blender, combine the capers, garlic, oregano, sardines and 2 tablespoons of the olive oil. Process until blended. Add the olives and process to form a coarse purée. Adjust the seasoning and transfer to a small bowl.

❧ Using a zester or a fine-holed shredder, shred the zest (yellow part only) from the lemon directly onto the olive purée (see glossary, page 126). Set aside.

❧ Prepare the crostini as directed and set aside to cool slightly.

❧ Pick over the arugula and discard any old leaves and the stems. Rinse and dry thoroughly, tear into small pieces and place in a large bowl.

❧ In a small bowl, combine the wine vinegar and salt. Stir to dissolve the salt. Sprinkle the vinegar over the greens and toss lightly until the leaves are coated. In the same small bowl, stir together the walnut oil and the remaining 2 tablespoons olive oil. While tossing the greens, drizzle on the oils. Continue to toss just until the leaves are lightly coated. Season to taste with pepper.

❧ To serve, divide the greens among salad plates. Spread the crostini generously with the olive purée and place 3 or 4 crostini on the side of each plate. Serve immediately.

SERVES 4

NOTES

A memorable first course for a dinner party, this salad may also be served for lunch along with a bowl of soup. The crostini make good hors d'oeuvres served with drinks as well.

In Italy the black olive purée that tops crostini usually includes anchovies, but I've found that sardines work equally well and appeal more to American tastes. The purée can be made a day ahead and refrigerated. Bring it to room temperature before using; assemble the crostini just before serving so they'll be at their most crisp.

Arugula leaves, with their slight edge of bitterness, are an excellent choice for the salad. If you can't find arugula, watercress is a good substitute. The most flavorful walnut oil for the dressing is the kind pressed from lightly toasted nuts. Refrigerate the oil once it has been opened.

FARFALLE WITH TUNA AND BLACK OLIVES

NOTES

This southern Italian pasta dish is one of the best of the region. The butterfly-shaped farfalle is especially pretty, but you can substitute other pasta of similar size. Look for imported Italian tuna packed in olive oil in well-stocked food stores or Italian markets, or use one of the good-quality Alaskan or north Atlantic brands.

Fresh dill or mint can take the place of the basil. For extra color, add red bell pepper (capsicum) to the sauce: cut the pepper into ½-inch (12-mm) squares and blanch in boiling water for 5 minutes before sautéing it with the green onion.

¼ cup (2 fl oz/60 ml) olive oil
4 or 5 green (spring) onions, including some tender green tops, chopped (about ¼ cup/¾ oz/20 g)
1 lemon
12 large fresh basil leaves, finely shredded, plus extra basil leaves for garnish
20 European black olives, such as Gaeta, Kalamata or Spanish, preferably pitted
1 can (12½ oz/390 g) solid-pack tuna in olive oil, preferably imported Italian, drained and flaked
Salt and freshly ground pepper
¾ lb (375 g) dried farfalle

In a large saucepan over medium-low heat, warm the olive oil. Add the green onions and sauté, stirring, until translucent, about 2 minutes. Using a zester or a fine-holed shredder, shred the zest (yellow part only) from the lemon directly onto the onions (see glossary, page 126). Add the shredded basil and the olives and stir to mix. Add the tuna and then cut the lemon in half and squeeze a little juice over the mixture to taste. Season to taste with salt and pepper and stir until well heated. Set aside and cover to keep warm.

🌿 Meanwhile, fill a large pot three-fourths full of water and bring to a rolling boil over high heat. Add the pasta and 1 tablespoon salt, stirring as you do, and boil until *al dente* (tender but still firm to the bite), about 8 minutes, or according to the package instructions.

🌿 Drain the pasta and immediately add it to the warm tuna-olive mixture; act quickly so that a little water is still clinging to the pasta. Toss well and briefly reheat for serving. Taste and adjust the seasoning.

🌿 Divide among warmed plates, garnish with the whole basil leaves and serve at once.

SERVES 4

BAKED SEMOLINA GNOCCHI

4 cups (32 fl oz/1 l) milk
½ teaspoon salt
Freshly ground pepper
Pinch of freshly grated nutmeg
1 cup (6 oz/185 g) semolina flour
1 tablespoon unsalted butter, plus ¼ cup (2 oz/60 g) unsalted butter, melted
⅔ cup (3 oz/90 g) freshly grated Italian Parmesan cheese, preferably
   Parmigiano-Reggiano
2 egg yolks, lightly beaten

In a deep, heavy saucepan over medium heat, warm the milk until small bubbles appear around the edges of the pan; do not allow to boil. Add the salt, pepper to taste and the nutmeg. Using a heavy whisk or wooden spoon to whisk or stir constantly, pour in the semolina slowly (to avoid lumping). Reduce the heat to low and continue to cook, stirring, until the mixture is very thick and stiff, 10–12 minutes. Be sure to scrape the bottom thoroughly while stirring, to avoid lumping or sticking.

🐚 Remove from the heat and add the 1 tablespoon butter; stir until fully melted and absorbed. Stir in ⅓ cup (1½ oz/45 g) of the Parmesan cheese until combined. Add the egg yolks and stir vigorously to keep the yolks from coagulating. Stir until well blended and smooth.

🐚 Using cold water, wet a jelly-roll (Swiss roll) pan or a 10-by-15-inch (25-by-37.5-cm) baking pan (this keeps the dough from sticking). Using a wet spatula or spoon, spread out the semolina mixture evenly in the pan. It should be approximately ¼ inch (6 mm) thick. Let cool completely, 40–50 minutes. On a warm day it is best to cover and refrigerate.

🐚 Position a rack in the upper part of an oven and preheat to 425°F (220°C). Generously butter a round 10-inch (25-cm) baking dish or a 9-by-11-inch (23-by-28-cm) rectangular or oval baking dish.

🐚 Using a round cutter 1½–2 inches (4–5 cm) in diameter, cut out rounds of the firm semolina. Place the rounds in a single layer in the baking dish, overlapping them slightly. Gather up the scraps, cut out additional rounds and add to the dish. Using a spoon, distribute the melted butter evenly over the rounds. Sprinkle the remaining ⅓ cup (1½ oz/45 g) cheese evenly over the top.

🐚 Bake until the top is golden and the butter is bubbly, about 15 minutes. Transfer the gnocchi to warmed plates and serve immediately.

SERVES 4

NOTES

After the publication of Marcella Hazan's first great book, *The Classic Italian Cook Book,* in 1976, many people (myself included) learned more than they'd ever expected to know about the marvelous food of northern Italy. One of the things I learned was how to make semolina gnocchi as made in Rome, and for quite a while I was preparing this dish about once a week.

Of all the gnocchi dishes, I think this one is probably the easiest and best. It's splendid as a dinner party first course, or as a brunch main course accompanied with a green salad. The gnocchi can be made in advance and refrigerated; just slip the dish into the oven 15 minutes before serving.

Semolina flour is finely ground from durum wheat—the wheat used for the finest pastas—and it cooks to a velvety consistency. Look for semolina imported from Italy. Or use stone-ground semolina from one of the many small mills in America; they are producing excellent flours that can be found in specialty-food stores.

NOTES

On my yearly buying trips to Paris and London in the early 1960s, I enjoyed many pleasant evenings sharing a bottle of wine and talking about food with the now-departed great English food writer Elizabeth David. On one of those evenings, she explained to me the essentials of this recipe. I've never forgotten them, have made this recipe many times and have always found the ravioli excellent. I have, however, updated the recipe by mixing it in a food processor.

The use of boiling water, instead of egg, makes a more pliable dough that is much easier to roll out. I think you will find these ravioli very easy to make.

A good cheese shop will carry at least one of the softer cheeses you will need—provolone, fontal or Fontina—as well as high-quality Parmesan.

The ravioli can be made a few hours ahead and refrigerated, if necessary. Drape a piece of plastic wrap over them to keep them from drying out.

CHEESE AND BASIL RAVIOLI

½ cup (2 oz/60 g) walnut pieces, coarsely chopped
1 egg
1½ cups (6 oz/185 g) freshly grated Italian Parmesan cheese, preferably Parmigiano-Reggiano
1½ cups (6 oz/185 g) shredded provolone, fontal or Fontina cheese
1½ tablespoons chopped fresh basil, plus 10–12 basil leaves, finely shredded, for garnish
Freshly ground pepper
2 pinches of freshly grated nutmeg
¼–⅓ cup (2–3 fl oz/60–80 ml) milk
Ravioli dough *(recipe on page 119)*
2 tablespoons unsalted butter
1 cup (8 fl oz/250 ml) heavy (double) cream
Salt

Preheat an oven to 325°F (165°C). Spread the walnuts on a baking sheet and bake until the nuts begin to change color and are fragrant, about 10 minutes; do not allow to brown too much. Remove from the oven and let cool.

In a bowl, beat the egg until blended. Add 1 cup (4 oz/125 g) of the Parmesan cheese; the provolone, fontal or Fontina cheese; the 1½ tablespoons chopped basil; pepper to taste and the nutmeg. Mix well. Stir in ¼ cup (2 fl oz/ 60 ml) milk to make a creamy but not runny mixture, adding more milk as needed to achieve the correct consistency. Set aside.

Prepare the ravioli dough, then roll out and fill as directed using the cheese mixture.

In a large frying pan over medium heat, melt the butter. Add the cream and heat, stirring, until slightly thickened. Season to taste with salt and pepper. Set aside and cover to keep warm.

Fill a large pot three-fourths full of water and bring to a rapid boil over high heat. Add 1 tablespoon salt and carefully slide in the ravioli. Cook until the ravioli rise to the surface and puff, 3–4 minutes. Using a slotted spoon, transfer the ravioli to the sauce in the frying pan.

Return the frying pan to medium heat and spoon the sauce over the ravioli until well coated and the sauce is thickened. Transfer to a warmed serving platter or individual warmed plates. Top evenly with the walnuts and shredded basil. Sprinkle with some of the remaining ½ cup (2 oz/60 g) Parmesan cheese and pass the rest at the table.

MAKES 48–64 RAVIOLI; SERVES 4–6

Fettuccine with Asparagus and Arugula

Both asparagus and arugula are beloved by northern Italians, who have created many different ways to serve them. In this recipe they are married in an excellent sauce for the popular pasta ribbons known as fettuccine. The slight bitterness of the arugula leaves provides a nice balance to the sweetness of the asparagus and cream. A touch of lemon juice and zest, added just before serving, contributes an extra dimension of freshness.

I have found that pasta is best when served quite hot. See page 125 for other tips on draining, saucing and serving pasta.

1 lb (500 g) asparagus, preferably small, slender spears
1 bunch arugula (rocket), 4–5 oz (125–155 g)
2 tablespoons olive oil
4 or 5 green (spring) onions, including some tender green tops, coarsely chopped (about ¼ cup/1¼ oz/37 g)
¾ cup (6 fl oz/180 ml) heavy (double) cream
Freshly grated nutmeg
Salt and freshly ground pepper
¾–1 lb (375–500 g) dried fettuccine
2 lemons

Break or cut off any tough white ends of the asparagus spears and discard. If medium-sized or larger, peel the spears as well: using a vegetable peeler or asparagus peeler and starting about 2 inches (5 cm) below the tip, peel off the thin outer skin from each spear. Cut on the diagonal into 1-inch (2.5-cm) lengths. You should have 2–2½ cups (8–10 oz/250–315 g). Set aside.

Pick over the arugula, discarding any old leaves and the stems. Rinse and drain well. Pat dry 4 leaves to use for garnish and set aside. Tear or cut the remaining leaves into bite-sized pieces. You should have 2–2½ cups (2–2½ oz/60–75 g), loosely packed. Set aside.

In a large saucepan over medium-low heat, warm the olive oil. Add the green onions and sauté gently, stirring, until translucent, 1–2 minutes. Add the cream, a sprinkling of nutmeg, and salt and pepper to taste. Set aside; cover to keep warm.

Meanwhile, fill a large pot three-fourths full of water and bring to a rolling boil over high heat. Add the fettuccine and 1 tablespoon salt, stirring as you do. Boil for about 2 minutes. Add the asparagus and arugula and continue to boil until the fettuccine and asparagus are *al dente* (tender but still firm to the bite), another 6–7 minutes. Drain and immediately add to the pan holding the cream mixture; act quickly so that a little water is still clinging to the pasta. Toss well. Taste and adjust the seasoning.

Divide the pasta among warmed plates. Using a zester or fine-holed shredder, shred the zest (yellow part only) from 1 of the lemons directly onto the pasta (see glossary, page 126).

Sprinkle a little nutmeg over each plate of pasta and garnish with the 4 reserved arugula leaves, tearing each leaf into small pieces. Cut the remaining lemon into wedges and place in a small bowl. Serve the pasta immediately, accompanied with the lemon wedges for diners to season to taste.

SERVES 4

POLENTA WITH PARMESAN CHEESE

7 cups (56 fl oz/1.75 l) water
2 teaspoons salt
2 cups (12 oz/375 g) Italian polenta
¼ cup (2 oz/60 g) unsalted butter, cut into small cubes
1 cup (4 oz/125 g) freshly grated Italian Parmesan cheese,
   preferably Parmigiano-Reggiano

In a deep, heavy saucepan over high heat, bring the water to a rapid boil. Add the salt and, while stirring continuously with a long-handled wooden spoon, gradually add the polenta in a thin, steady stream until all has been incorporated. Continuing to stir constantly to keep lumps from forming, reduce the heat until the mixture only bubbles occasionally. Continue to cook, stirring, until thick, smooth and creamy, 20–25 minutes; be careful to scrape the bottom and sides of the pan to avoid sticking or lumping. The polenta will start to come away from the sides of the pan and the spoon should stand upright alone.

❧ Remove from the heat and stir in the butter, a few cubes at a time, until fully absorbed. Then stir in ½ cup (2 oz/60 g) of the Parmesan cheese. Return the pan to the heat for a few seconds, continuing to stir, until the polenta is piping hot.

❧ Transfer to a warmed bowl or platter and serve immediately, with the remaining Parmesan cheese in a small bowl alongside.

MAKES ABOUT 8 CUPS (4 LB/2 KG); SERVES 4–6

TO MAKE POLENTA CROSTINI:
On a baking sheet, spread out the cooked hot polenta about ¼ inch (6 mm) thick. Set aside until cold and set, 30–40 minutes, or refrigerate. Preheat a broiler (griller). Cut the polenta into 1½-by-2½-inch (4-by-6-cm) rectangles or 2-inch (5-cm) rounds. Brush each side with olive oil and place on a baking sheet. Place under the broiler until golden and crispy, 3–4 minutes on each side. Serve as an appetizer or to accompany soup or salad.

TO MAKE FRIED POLENTA SQUARES:
On a baking sheet, spread out the cooked hot polenta ½ inch (12 mm) thick. Set aside until cold and set, 30–40 minutes, or refrigerate. Cut into 3- or 4-inch (7.5- or 10-cm) squares. In a sauté pan over medium heat, warm 3 tablespoons olive oil. When hot, add several polenta squares and fry until golden, 4–5 minutes on each side. Sprinkle with coarse salt. Transfer to a serving plate, then fry the remaining squares. Serve as an accompaniment to meat, poultry or fish.

A richly textured, flavorful dish of cooked cornmeal, polenta is one of the great traditions of northern Italian cooking. To be truly first-rate, however, it needs to be cooked slowly, with almost constant stirring, resulting in a soft, creamy consistency. The addition of butter and good Parmesan cheese enhances the richness and smoothness of the polenta, yielding a dish that is as perfect with a rustic stew as it is with fried eggs and ham at a weekend brunch.

Imported Italian long-cooking polenta is the best. It is evenly and finely ground and cooks to a smooth, even consistency.

I also offer two variations for cooked polenta—baked polenta crostini and fried polenta squares.

PENNE WITH TOMATO AND BROCCOLI

I can't imagine an easier or tastier pasta dish, or one that makes a simpler, prettier picture than this combination of quill-shaped pasta tubes, bright red tomatoes and small green florets of broccoli. The tomato sauce cooks within 15 minutes, and the pasta and broccoli can be prepared while the sauce finishes simmering. Of course, you'll find the sauce will be at its best in high summer, when tomatoes are at their freshest, firmest and most flavorful.

If you can't find fresh oregano, use ½ teaspoon dried oregano. And feel free to leave out the bacon, if you prefer.

1½ lb (750 g) ripe plum (Roma) tomatoes
1 bunch broccoli, about 1½ lb (750 g)
3 oz (90 g) thickly sliced lean bacon (2 or 3 slices), cut crosswise
   into pieces ¼ inch (6 mm) wide
2 cloves garlic, chopped
¼ cup (1 oz/30 g) chopped yellow onion
1 teaspoon minced fresh oregano
Pinch of red pepper flakes
Salt
¾–1 lb (375–500 g) dried penne or rigatoni
½ cup (2 oz/60 g) freshly grated Italian Parmesan cheese,
   preferably Parmigiano-Reggiano

Core and peel the tomatoes (see glossary, page 124). Cut the tomatoes in half crosswise and carefully squeeze out the seeds. Chop the tomatoes coarsely; you should have about 3 cups (18 oz/560 g). Set aside.

❧ Remove the florets from the broccoli stalks; reserve the stalks for another use. Break or cut apart the florets so they are uniform in size. Set aside.

❧ In a large saucepan or frying pan over medium-low heat, sauté the bacon until crisp, 3–4 minutes. Pour off the fat, but leave the bacon in the pan. Add the garlic and onion and sauté gently over medium-low heat, stirring occasionally, until the onion is translucent, 4–5 minutes. Add the tomatoes, oregano and red pepper flakes and raise the heat to medium. Continue to cook, stirring occasionally, until the tomatoes have softened, 8–10 minutes longer. Season to taste with salt.

❧ Meanwhile, fill a large pot three-fourths full of water and bring to a rolling boil over high heat. Add the pasta and 1 tablespoon salt, stirring as you do, and cook at a rapid boil for about 4 minutes. Add the broccoli and boil until the pasta and broccoli are *al dente* (tender but still firm to the bite), another 4–5 minutes.

❧ Drain the pasta and broccoli and immediately add to the pan holding the tomatoes; act quickly so that a little water is still clinging to the pasta. Toss well; the pasta will continue to absorb liquid.

❧ Divide the pasta among warmed plates and sprinkle with some of the grated Parmesan cheese. Serve immediately, with the remaining cheese in a small bowl alongside.

SERVES 4

SAFFRON RISOTTO WITH CRAB

1 bunch of small leaf spinach, 4–5 oz (125–155 g)
2 cups (16 fl oz/500 ml) bottled clam juice
2 cups (16 fl oz/500 ml) water
½ teaspoon saffron threads
Salt
¼ cup (2 oz/60 g) unsalted butter
1 small yellow onion, finely chopped (about ½ cup/2 oz/60 g)
1½ cups (10½ oz/330 g) Italian Arborio rice or medium-grain white rice
1 cup (8 fl oz/250 ml) dry white wine
1 tablespoon dry Marsala
Freshly ground pepper
½ lb (250 g) fresh-cooked crab meat, picked over for any cartilage or shell fragments and flaked
2 tablespoons fresh lemon juice
Chopped fresh flat-leaf (Italian) parsley, optional

Wash the spinach carefully, drain well and remove the stems. Pick out about 20 of the smallest leaves; reserve the rest for another use. Wrap the leaves in a damp kitchen towel and set aside. Combine the clam juice and water in a saucepan to form a broth and heat to just below boiling. Keep hot.

❧ To draw out the flavor of the saffron, place the saffron threads and a pinch of salt in a large metal spoon and hold over heat until warmed, just a few seconds. Using a teaspoon, crush the saffron threads to a powder. Place in a small bowl, add ½ cup (4 fl oz/125 ml) of the hot broth and set aside.

❧ In a large, heavy saucepan over medium-low heat, melt the butter. Add the onion and sauté, stirring, until translucent, 4–5 minutes. Add the rice and stir until coated with the butter and becoming opaque, about 2 minutes. Reduce the heat to low, add the white wine and stir until the liquid has been absorbed, 3–4 minutes. Stir in the saffron broth and cook until absorbed, another 2 minutes.

❧ Start adding the hot broth, ½ cup (4 fl oz/125 ml) at a time, while stirring. Cook slowly, stirring frequently, until the liquid has been completely absorbed before adding the next batch of broth. The risotto is ready when it is creamy and the grains are tender but slightly *al dente* (still firm to the bite) in the center. This will take 25–30 minutes; you may not need all of the liquid.

❧ Stir in the Marsala and salt and pepper to taste. Then gently stir in the crab and finally the lemon juice. Taste for seasoning. Add more liquid if necessary.

❧ To serve, arrange the spinach leaves on warmed plates or in shallow bowls, creating a bed for the risotto. Spoon the risotto in a mound on the spinach. Garnish with the parsley, if desired, and serve immediately.

SERVES 4

NOTES

At a good restaurant in Italy, risotto can be absolute heaven—silky smooth and creamy, with a slight bite to each rice grain and the distinctive influence of other ingredients. No wonder people are willing to endure the 25–30 minutes of stirring required to coax the starch from the plump grains of Arborio rice.

For this risotto, it is best to use Arborio rice imported from Italy. I've included saffron and crab—two flavors that blend well with the rich, creamy rice. Plan your menu so that other dishes can be cooked ahead, freeing you to pay full attention to the risotto for the last half hour or so. The dish must be served and eaten at the moment the rice reaches the *al dente* stage—tender and cooked through, yet still pleasingly chewy.

For the best taste and consistency, purchase fresh-cooked crab meat. If there is no crab at the market, buy medium-sized shrimp (prawns), then peel, devein and cook them before adding to the risotto.

ROASTED ROSEMARY CHICKEN

One of Italy's favorite herbs, rosemary has such a pronounced flavor that it is commonly used in moderation. But when it seasons a chicken for roasting, somehow more can be added, yielding wonderfully aromatic results.

Seek out a fresh free-range chicken—that is, one that has been raised in open areas and fed a good natural diet. They are not hard to find these days, and they have a much better flavor than factory-raised birds. Take care not to overcook the chicken. Start testing the breast and thigh for doneness after about 50 minutes of roasting. The breast naturally cooks in less time, so positioning the bird on its side for part of the roasting exposes the thighs to more heat, ensuring that the bird cooks more evenly.

There are different theories on the proper oven temperature for roasting a chicken. For a small chicken (3–4 lb/1.5–2 kg), a higher temperature works well. I have always attained very moist results by roasting in a 425°F (220°C) oven.

I like to serve the roasted chicken with golden polenta crostini (see page 45).

1 chicken, 3½–4½ lb (1.75–2.25 kg), preferably free-range
1 lemon, quartered
Salt
3 cloves garlic, unpeeled
7 fresh rosemary sprigs
Extra-virgin olive oil
Freshly ground pepper
2 cups (16 fl oz/500 ml) water

Position a rack in the lower part of an oven and preheat to 425°F (220°C).

❧ Discard the giblets and neck, if any, from the chicken, or reserve for another use. Remove any fat from around the cavity. Rinse the chicken inside and out. Dry with paper towels. Rub the cavity with 1 of the lemon quarters and leave it in the cavity. Sprinkle the cavity lightly with salt. Using the flat side of a large knife, smash the garlic cloves and then peel them. Place inside the cavity along with the remaining 3 lemon quarters and 3 of the rosemary sprigs. Close the cavity with a small skewer or wooden toothpick.

❧ Place one of the remaining rosemary sprigs under each wing and one between each leg and the body of the chicken. Truss the chicken: using kitchen string, tie the legs together and then tie the legs and wings close to the body. Brush the chicken with olive oil and sprinkle with salt and pepper.

❧ Oil a rack in a roasting pan and place the chicken, on its side, on the rack. Add 1 cup (8 fl oz/250 ml) of the water to the pan. Place in the oven and roast for 20 minutes. Turn the chicken over onto its other side, brush with olive oil and roast for another 20 minutes. Turn the chicken breast-side up, brush with oil again and roast another 20 minutes, basting a couple of times with the pan juices. Check if the chicken is done by inserting an instant-read thermometer into the thickest part of the breast or thigh away from the bone. It should read about 165°F (74°C) in the breast or 180°F (82°C) in the thigh. Remove from the oven when it is within 2–3 degrees of the desired temperature, as it will continue to cook from its internal heat. (Alternatively, pierce the thigh joint with a knife tip; the juices should run clear.) Transfer to a warmed serving platter and cover loosely with aluminum foil for 10 minutes before carving.

❧ Using a spoon, skim the fat from the pan juices and discard. Place the pan over medium heat. Add the remaining 1 cup (8 fl oz/250 ml) water to the pan and heat, stirring to dislodge any browned-on bits from the pan bottom. Simmer for 1–2 minutes, continuing to stir. Season to taste with salt and pepper.

❧ Carve the chicken and spoon some of the juices over each serving.

SERVES 4

SAUTÉED CHICKEN BREASTS WITH PARMESAN CHEESE

NOTES

Thin, golden crusts of Parmesan cheese seal in the juices of these pan-cooked chicken breasts. Good-quality Parmesan will produce the finest dish.

Dry white vermouth adds a hint of intriguing flavor to the sauce, but any dry white wine can be substituted. Be sure to let the sauce boil for a few seconds to evaporate the alcohol.

Serve this simple main course alongside your favorite vegetable. Baked Stuffed Tomatoes with Basil (recipe on page 99) or Italian Green Beans with Mint (page 86) are good choices.

4 chicken breast halves, about 10 oz (315 g) each, skinned and boned
  (about 6 oz/185 g each, if buying boneless breasts)
¼ cup (1 oz/30 g) freshly grated Italian Parmesan cheese,
  preferably Parmigiano-Reggiano
2 tablespoons all-purpose (plain) flour
Salt and freshly ground pepper
2 tablespoons unsalted butter
2 tablespoons olive oil
⅓ cup (3 fl oz/80 ml) dry white vermouth
2–3 tablespoons capers, rinsed and drained

Remove any excess fat from the chicken breasts. Rinse and pat dry with paper towels. Place each breast between 2 sheets of waxed paper and, using a rolling pin, flatten the breasts to an even thickness. On a plate, combine the Parmesan cheese, flour and a little salt and pepper. Stir until well mixed. Coat each breast evenly with the cheese mixture. Set aside.

In a large sauté pan or frying pan over medium-high heat, melt the butter with the olive oil. When hot, add the chicken breasts to the pan, in 2 batches if necessary to avoid crowding, and sauté, turning once, until golden and cooked through, 4–5 minutes on each side. To test, pierce the breasts with the tip of a sharp knife; the juices should run clear. Transfer to a warmed serving platter or to individual warmed plates.

Pour off any excess fat from the pan and return to medium heat. Add the vermouth, stirring to dislodge any browned-on bits from the pan bottom. Add the capers and boil for a few seconds.

Spoon the caper sauce over the chicken breasts and serve immediately.

SERVES 4

BAKED CHICKEN WITH ARTICHOKES

3 lemons
10 baby artichokes, about 1 lb (500 g) total weight
1 chicken, 3–3½ lb (1.5–1.75 kg), preferably free-range, cut into serving pieces
1 tablespoon unsalted butter
1 tablespoon olive oil
8 fresh sage leaves
2 large shallots, chopped
¼ cup (2 fl oz/60 ml) dry white wine or water
Salt and freshly ground pepper

Position a rack in the center of an oven and preheat to 425°F (220°C).

❧ Squeeze the juice from 1 of the lemons into a medium-sized bowl. Trim the artichokes (see glossary, page 126). Cut in half lengthwise and immediately put into the bowl of lemon juice. Toss to coat the cut surfaces with the juice.

❧ Fill a large saucepan half full of water and bring to a boil. Add the artichokes and lemon juice, reduce the heat to medium-high and cook, uncovered, until almost tender when pierced with a knife tip, 5–6 minutes. Drain and set aside.

❧ Trim any excess fat from the chicken pieces. Cut each breast half crosswise into 2 pieces. Discard the chicken back, neck and giblets (if any) or save for another use. Cut off the wing tips and discard.

❧ In a large sauté pan over medium-high heat, melt the butter with the olive oil. When hot, add the chicken pieces, in 2 batches if necessary to avoid crowding, and brown lightly on both sides, turning once, 4–5 minutes on each side. Using tongs, transfer to a baking dish or pan, skin side down. Tuck 4 of the sage leaves under the chicken pieces.

❧ Reduce the heat under the sauté pan to medium-low and add the shallots. Sauté gently until translucent, 2–3 minutes. Add the wine or water, stirring to dislodge any browned-on bits. Bring to a boil, raising the heat if necessary, and pour over the chicken. Cut another lemon in half and squeeze the juice from one of the lemon halves over the chicken. Season to taste with salt and pepper.

❧ Bake for 20 minutes, basting several times. Turn the chicken over, skin side up, add the artichoke halves and continue to bake, basting occasionally, until the chicken and artichokes are tender, 20–30 minutes longer. To test, cut into the chicken; it should be opaque throughout and the juices should run clear.

❧ Using tongs, transfer the chicken and artichokes to a warmed serving dish. If necessary, place the pan over high heat to thicken the juices. Season to taste with lemon juice from the remaining cut half and salt and pepper. Pour the juices over the chicken. Using a zester or fine-holed shredder, shred the zest (yellow part only) from the remaining lemon directly onto the chicken pieces (see glossary, page 126). Garnish with the remaining 4 sage leaves. Serve immediately.

SERVES 4

A dish you are apt to encounter in a country restaurant in Tuscany, this hearty main course would be a good choice for a weekend dinner. The combination of lemon and sage is quintessentially Mediterranean.

Fresh baby artichokes, especially available in spring, are well worth the little time their preparation takes. Choose small, solid, compact ones—certain signs that they are young and tender. If fresh are unavailable, the dish will work with frozen artichokes.

If you've never used fresh sage before, you'll find it a great improvement over its dried counterpart—and nothing at all like the flavor of typical poultry-seasoning mixes. You might even try growing the herb in your garden.

For the best flavor, get a fresh free-range chicken from your poultry market.

NOTES

Braised Chicken with Eggplant and Orange

The aromatic, sweet flavors of this southern Italian dish—tomato, eggplant, black olives, marjoram and orange—reflect the exotic influence of North Africa. It goes very well with mashed potatoes or egg noodles.

For the most healthful results, trim off any excess fat from the chicken pieces before cooking them. When I cut up a chicken, I always make a little broth by combining the back, neck, giblets (not the liver) and wing tips in a saucepan with water to cover, a piece of yellow onion and celery, a bay leaf, 2 fresh thyme sprigs and salt and freshly ground pepper to taste. I simmer the broth for about 45 minutes, then strain it and use it for soups and sauces.

Gaeta, Kalamata or Spanish olives will impart a distinctive flavor to the dish. As these olives are pre-served in brine, you may find them too salty, in which case rinse and drain them. Or soak them in water for 30 minutes, then drain.

If fresh marjoram is unavailable, substitute fresh oregano, mint, basil or dill, or 1 teaspoon dried marjoram.

1 globe eggplant (aubergine), about 1 lb (500 g), unpeeled
Salt
1½ lb (750 g) ripe plum (Roma) tomatoes
1 chicken, 3½–4 lb (1.75–2 kg), preferably free-range, cut into serving pieces
3 tablespoons olive oil
2 large cloves garlic, thinly sliced (about 2 tablespoons)
2 teaspoons chopped fresh marjoram
1 orange
Freshly ground pepper
½ cup (2½ oz/75 g) European black olives *(see note)*
Coarsely chopped flat-leaf (Italian) parsley for garnish

Cut the eggplant into 1-inch (2.5-cm) cubes and place in a colander. Sprinkle with salt, tossing them to mix evenly. Place the colander over a bowl for about 1 hour to drain the bitter juices. Rinse and drain. Set aside.

Meanwhile, core and peel the tomatoes (see glossary, page 124). Cut in half crosswise and squeeze out the seeds. Chop the tomatoes coarsely; you should have about 3 cups (18 oz/560 g). Set aside.

Trim any excess fat from the chicken pieces. Cut each breast-half crosswise into 2 pieces. Cut off the wing tips and discard, along with the back, neck and giblets (if any), or save for another use (see note).

In a large sauté pan over medium-high heat, warm the olive oil. When hot, add the chicken pieces, in 2 batches if necessary to avoid crowding, and lightly brown on both sides, 4–5 minutes on each side. Transfer to a plate. Reduce the heat to medium-low, add the garlic and sauté gently, stirring, until it just starts to change color, 1–2 minutes. Add the tomatoes and marjoram and cook, stirring occasionally, for 2–3 minutes. Return the chicken to the pan.

Using a zester or fine-holed shredder, shred the zest (orange part only) from the orange directly onto the chicken (see glossary, page 126). Then squeeze enough juice to measure ½ cup (4 fl oz/125 ml). Pour over the chicken and season with salt and pepper. Arrange the eggplant cubes and the olives over the chicken.

Cover and simmer over low heat for 30 minutes. Using tongs, rearrange the chicken to mix in the eggplant and olives. Cover partially and simmer until tender, about 30 minutes longer. To test, cut into the chicken; it should be opaque throughout and the juices should run clear. Adjust the seasoning.

To serve, arrange the chicken pieces on a warmed platter and spoon the tomato mixture over the top. Garnish with chopped parsley and serve at once.

SERVES 4

BOILED CHICKEN AND HAM

3 cups (24 fl oz/750 ml) chicken broth
2 cups (16 fl oz/500 ml) dry white wine
1 chicken, 3½–4 lb (1.75–2 kg), preferably free-range
1 medium-sized yellow onion, quartered
1 carrot, peeled and cut into 2-inch (5-cm) lengths
1 celery stalk, cut into 2-inch (5-cm) lengths
1 or 2 cloves garlic
1 piece boneless lean smoked ham, 1–1½ lb (500–750 g), about 2½ inches
  (6 cm) thick (or 1½–2 lb/750 g–1 kg with bone), trimmed of fat
Boiling water, as needed
1 bay leaf
2 or 3 fresh marjoram sprigs or 1 teaspoon dried marjoram
3 or 4 whole peppercorns
2 tablespoons unsalted butter
2 tablespoons all-purpose (plain) flour
½ cup (4 fl oz/125 ml) heavy (double) cream, or as needed
1–2 teaspoons fresh lemon juice
Salt and freshly ground pepper

Combine the broth and wine in a saucepan and heat almost to a boil. Remove any fat from the chicken cavity, rinse inside and out and pat dry. Place the onion, carrot, celery and garlic in the cavity and secure closed with a small skewer. Truss the chicken: using kitchen string, tie the legs and wings close to the body.

In a deep pot just large enough to accommodate them, place the chicken, breast side up, and the ham. Add the broth mixture and enough of the boiling water just to cover the chicken. Place the bay leaf, marjoram and peppercorns on a small square of cheesecloth (muslin). Tie the edges together with string and add to the pot. Bring to a boil, skimming off any froth. Reduce the heat to low, cover tightly and barely simmer, skimming occasionally, until the chicken is tender, about 1 hour. To test, cut into the thigh or breast; it should be opaque throughout and the juices should run clear. Remove from the heat, skim off any fat from the liquid and set aside, partially covered.

In a small saucepan over medium heat, melt the butter. Add the flour and stir and cook until the mixture begins to color, 1–2 minutes. Slowly whisk in 1 cup (8 fl oz/250 ml) of the liquid from the chicken pot. Whisk until thickened and smooth, about 2 minutes. Whisk in the ½ cup (4 fl oz/125 ml) cream and 1 teaspoon of the lemon juice, adding more cream or broth if needed to thin slightly. Season to taste with salt, pepper and more lemon juice, if necessary.

To serve, transfer the chicken and ham to a warmed platter. Carve the chicken and slice the ham. Serve the lemon sauce alongside.

SERVES 4–6

NOTES

Italy's *bollito misto*—a mixed boiled dinner that might include chicken, ham, sausages and other meats—is one of the country's most satisfying rustic dishes. This short version offers all the satisfaction with considerably less effort.

The chunk of ham contributes a delicious accent to the chicken; the two meats go together particularly well. Cook them at a bare simmer (with just a few bubbles rising to the surface) until just tender; any faster and longer and they will dry out. Technically, the recipe should be called "poached" rather than "boiled."

Be sure to seek out a free-range chicken for this dish. They are available at most poultry shops and better food stores.

I like to serve the meat in a deep dish with some of the cooking broth, accompanied by steamed vegetables.

VEAL SCALOPPINE WITH MARSALA

NOTES

Thin scallops of veal are one of the most popular and typical main courses of Italy—and one of the best, especially when accented with fresh sage. The only veal that works well for this purpose comes from a truly young animal; otherwise, the meat is likely to be tough. Seek out a good butcher who stocks the best-quality veal and who knows how to prepare scallops the right way: each scallop should be no more than 4–6 inches (10–15 cm) square, weighing 1½–2 ounces (45–60 g) and pounded to a thickness of ¼ inch (6 mm) or less.

Cooking the scaloppine successfully depends upon having hot oil in a large pan and searing the meat quickly. Longer cooking will toughen the veal. The sauce is then prepared very quickly, so the veal has no time to cool.

This timing requires a little practice, but once it is achieved you will have mastered a quick and elegant dish.

12–16 thin veal scallops, 1½–2 oz (45–60 g) each
½ cup (2½ oz/75 g) all-purpose (plain) flour
3–4 tablespoons vegetable oil
12 fresh sage leaves, plus extra for garnish
⅓ cup (3 fl oz/80 ml) dry Marsala, preferably Italian
2 tablespoons unsalted butter
Salt and freshly ground pepper
Lemon slices for garnish

Trim off any excess fat or any thin white skin remaining on the edges of the veal scallops. Using a sharp knife, make 3 or 4 small cuts around the edge of each scallop, to help keep them flat while cooking. Place each scallop between 2 sheets of waxed paper or plastic wrap and, using a meat pounder or the side of a heavy cleaver blade, pound to flatten to an even thickness of ⅛–¼ inch (3–6 mm). (Or ask your butcher to do this step.) Pat dry with paper towels.

Spread out the flour on a large plate. Dip half of the veal scallops in the flour, coating them evenly and shaking off any excess. In a large sauté pan or frying pan over high heat, warm 3 tablespoons of the oil. When hot but not smoking, add the flour-coated slices to the pan, along with half of the sage leaves. Sear the meat quickly, turning once, until lightly browned, 40–50 seconds on each side. Transfer the veal to a warmed plate, along with the sage leaves. Repeat with the remaining veal scallops and sage leaves, adding more oil to the pan if necessary.

Pour off the oil in the pan. Place the pan over high heat and add the Marsala. Cook, stirring to dislodge any browned-on bits, until reduced and thickened, 2–3 minutes. Add the butter and stir until blended. Season to taste with salt and pepper.

Return the meat, with any juices, and the sage leaves to the pan and turn the meat over twice to coat well with the sauce. Transfer the veal and sage leaves to a warmed serving platter or warmed individual plates and spoon the sauce on top. Garnish with fresh sage leaves and lemon slices. Serve immediately.

SERVES 4

BAKED PEPPERS STUFFED WITH ITALIAN SAUSAGE

4 medium-sized red bell peppers (capsicums), about 1 lb (500 g) total weight
4 ripe plum (Roma) tomatoes
2 tablespoons unsalted butter or olive oil
1 small yellow onion, diced (about ½ cup/2 oz/60 g)
1 celery stalk, trimmed and diced
4 fresh mild Italian sausages, about 1 lb (500 g) total weight, casings removed and meat crumbled into small chunks
8 European black olives, such as Gaeta, Kalamata or Spanish, pitted and chopped
Salt and freshly ground pepper
1 cup (2 oz/60 g) fresh bread crumbs
1 cup (8 fl oz/250 ml) hot tap water

Position a rack in the center of an oven and preheat to 375°F (190°C).

Carefully cut each pepper in half lengthwise. Remove the stem, being careful not to cut into the flesh. Remove the seeds and ribs. Fill a large saucepan three-fourths full of water and bring to a boil over medium-high heat. Add the pepper halves, bring the water back to a boil and parboil for 4–5 minutes. Using a slotted spoon, transfer the pepper halves to a colander to drain. Keep the water at a boil to peel the tomatoes.

Core and peel the tomatoes (see glossary, page 124). Cut in half crosswise and carefully squeeze out the seeds. Chop the tomatoes coarsely and set aside.

In a large sauté pan or frying pan over medium-low heat, warm the butter or olive oil. Add the onion and sauté, stirring, until translucent, 4–5 minutes. Add the celery and sauté until starting to soften, another 2–3 minutes. Using a slotted spoon, transfer the onion and celery to a plate. Set aside.

Add the crumbled sausage to the pan and sauté over medium heat, turning several times, until lightly browned, 8–10 minutes. Return the onion mixture to the pan along with the tomatoes. Mix together and continue to cook over medium heat for 3–4 minutes to blend the flavors. Stir in the olives and season to taste with salt and pepper.

Arrange the pepper halves, cut side up, in a baking dish in which they just fit comfortably in a single layer. Spoon the sausage mixture into the peppers, dividing it evenly. Top evenly with the bread crumbs. Add the hot water to the dish.

Bake, uncovered, until the crumbs are golden and the mixture is bubbly, about 40 minutes. Using a slotted spatula, transfer to warmed plates and serve immediately.

SERVES 4

Splendidly rustic, this dish can be assembled several hours ahead of time, refrigerated and then baked just before serving.

Some excellent fresh sausages are being made today by young chefs who have rediscovered the art of sausage making. Flavorful chicken or turkey sausages, for example, would be delectable in this colorful dish.

Serve the stuffed peppers for supper or a weekend lunch, accompanied by fried polenta (see page 45).

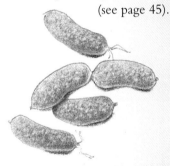

Some of the best pork dishes I've ever eaten have been in Italy, and pork loin flavored with fresh sage is among the most memorable. Today, pork is the product of new diets and more selective breeding than in the past, so the meat can be very low in fat, especially if you trim off any excess fat before cooking.

The pork loin may be a single piece of meat about 9 inches (23 cm) long, or it can be two shorter pieces tied together by the butcher. Joined with the fresh sage and garlic, balsamic vinegar contributes a slightly tart-sweet flavor that complements the meat. Any leftover pork can be thinly sliced and served cold.

BRAISED PORK LOIN WITH SAGE

2½–3 lb (1.25–1.5 kg) boneless center-cut pork loin *(see note)*
8 fresh sage leaves, plus sage leaves and sage blossoms for garnish (optional)
Salt and freshly ground pepper
3 tablespoons unsalted butter
1 tablespoon olive oil
2 cloves garlic, left whole
1 bay leaf
½ cup (4 fl oz/125 ml) dry white wine, or as needed
2 tablespoons balsamic vinegar
2 tablespoons all-purpose (plain) flour

Trim any excess fat from the pork loin. If the loin has not been tied by the butcher, tie it with kitchen string in 3 or 4 places. Place 6 of the sage leaves under the string, positioning 3 leaves evenly spaced on top and 3 on the bottom of the meat. Rub the meat all over with salt and pepper.

❧ Select a deep, heavy pot in which the pork loin will just fit comfortably. Place it over medium-high heat and add 2 tablespoons of the butter and the olive oil. When hot, add the pork loin and sear quickly to brown lightly on all sides, 5–6 minutes total. Reduce the heat to medium-low, add the garlic and sauté gently, stirring, until it just begins to change color, 1–2 minutes. Transfer the meat and garlic cloves to a plate. Pour off the fat from the pot.

❧ Return the meat to the pot. Tuck the garlic cloves under the meat, along with the bay leaf. Add the ½ cup (4 fl oz/125 ml) wine, the balsamic vinegar and the remaining 2 sage leaves. Cover tightly, reduce the heat to low and simmer gently until tender when pierced with a fork, 1½–2 hours; turn the roast over halfway through cooking. Add more wine, if needed, to maintain the level of liquid in the pot.

❧ Transfer the meat to a serving platter and cover with aluminum foil to keep warm. Remove the garlic cloves, bay leaf and sage from the pan juices and discard. Using a spoon, skim off any fat from the surface of the pan juices. Reserve the juices. You should have at least 1 cup (8 fl oz/250 ml); if you have less, add water as needed.

❧ To make the sauce, in a small saucepan over medium heat, melt the remaining 1 tablespoon butter. Add the flour and cook, stirring, for 1–2 minutes. Add the reserved pan juices, whisking constantly. Continue to whisk until thickened and smooth, 2–3 minutes. If the sauce is too thick, add water to achieve the desired consistency. Season to taste with salt and pepper.

❧ To serve, slice the meat and arrange it on the platter. Spoon the sauce over the slices and garnish with sage leaves and sage blossoms, if desired.

SERVES 4

BRAISED VEAL SHANKS

½ cup (2½ oz/75 g) all-purpose (plain) flour
8 veal shank (shin) pieces from foreleg, each 2½ inches (6 cm) thick and
    weighing 6–8 oz (185–250 g) each, or 4 veal shank pieces from hind leg,
    each 2 inches (5 cm) thick and weighing 10–12 oz (315–375 g)
2 tablespoons unsalted butter
2 tablespoons olive oil
¼ cup (2 fl oz/60 ml) Cognac
½ cup (4 fl oz/125 ml) beef broth
1 medium-sized yellow onion
½ teaspoon salt
Freshly ground pepper
1 teaspoon cornstarch (cornflour), if needed
1 lemon

Spread out the flour on a plate. Coat each veal shank piece evenly with the
flour, shaking off any excess. Select a large sauté pan or deep frying pan in which
the veal pieces will fit in a single layer. Place over medium-high heat and melt
the butter with the olive oil. When hot, add the veal pieces, cut side up, and
sauté until lightly browned on all sides, 6–8 minutes total. Arrange the pieces cut
side up and in a single layer, then remove from the heat.

❧ In a small pan over medium-low heat, warm the Cognac. Remove from the
heat. Well away from the heat, ignite the Cognac with a long match. Carefully
pour the flaming Cognac over the veal pieces. Let the flame burn itself out, then
return the pan to low heat. Add the broth, onion, the salt, and pepper to taste.
Cover and barely simmer until the veal is tender when pierced with a fork, 1¼–
1½ hours if using shank pieces from the foreleg and 1½–2 hours if using pieces
from the hind leg, turning the veal pieces over halfway through cooking. When
done, transfer the veal pieces, cut side up, to a serving platter. Set aside and
cover to keep warm.

❧ Remove the pan from the heat and, using a spoon, skim off any fat from the
surface of the liquid. Return the pan to high heat and boil the liquid until
thickened and reduced to about ½ cup (4 fl oz/125 ml). (Or thicken with cornstarch mixed with a little cold water.) Taste and adjust the seasoning. Pour the
sauce over the veal pieces.

❧ Using a zester or a fine-holed shredder, shred the zest (yellow part only) from
the lemon directly onto the veal (see glossary, page 126). Serve at once.

SERVES 4

This recipe for Italy's classic
osso buco was given to me in the
mid-1960s by a friend named
Valentina, an Italian couturier and
exceptionally good cook whose
salon was across the street from
Williams-Sonoma's first San
Francisco store. She didn't use the
typical seasoning ingredients for
this dish, relying instead on flaming
the meat with good Cognac after
browning, then adding an onion
and a little well-flavored beef broth
for slowly simmering the veal. The
results are at once delicate and
richly flavored.

Seek out a good butcher who
specializes in quality veal. The veal
shanks must come from a very
young animal and preferably from
the front shanks, which are smaller
and more tender. Only the center
two pieces of the shank should be
used; the end pieces contain too
much bone. The veal should be
pale pink and have no fat.

This dish is excellent served with
a simple risotto or egg noodles. Try
it with Saffron Risotto (follow the
recipe on page 49, leaving out the
Marsala, crab and
lemon juice).

BOILED BEEF WITH GREEN SAUCE

In Italy meat is often served boiled—that is, gently poached—with a tangy green herb sauce. The sauce I include here combines fresh parsley and sage with garlic, balsamic vinegar and olive oil, a blend that contrasts nicely with the beef. You can also offer the sauce with any cold sliced meats.

Simmer the beef very slowly for the moistest, most tender results. This is a good meal to prepare on a weekend, when you have a little extra time for the cooking. There may even be leftovers for another meal during the week.

1 lean beef brisket, 3–3½ lb (1.5–1.75 kg), preferably center cut
8 cups (64 fl oz/2 l) water
Salt
6 carrots, peeled and trimmed
6 celery stalks, trimmed
1 yellow onion, cut in half
2 cloves garlic, left whole
1 tablespoon balsamic vinegar
4 medium leeks
1 lemon
8 baby artichokes
Green sauce *(recipe on page 118)*

Trim any excess fat from the meat. Select a large, heavy pot in which the meat fits comfortably. Place it over medium-high heat, add the water and bring to a boil. Add 2 teaspoons salt and the meat. The water should just cover the meat; add more if necessary. Bring back to a boil and, using a skimmer or spoon, remove any froth that collects on the surface. Cut 1 of the carrots and 1 of the celery stalks into small pieces and add to the pot, along with the onion halves, garlic and balsamic vinegar. Reduce the heat to low, cover and barely simmer until the meat is almost tender when pierced with a fork, 2½–3 hours.

🌿 Meanwhile, trim the leeks, cutting off the root end and leaving some of the tender green top intact. Cut all the leeks to the same length. Starting at the top, make a shallow lengthwise slit along each leek to within 2 inches (5 cm) of the root end. Rinse away any dirt lodged between the leaves. Set aside.

🌿 Squeeze the juice from the lemon into a bowl of water large enough to hold the artichokes. Trim the artichokes (see glossary, page 126). Immediately put the artichokes into the bowl of lemon water. Set aside.

🌿 When the meat is almost done, remove and discard the onion halves and the carrot and celery pieces. Cut the 5 remaining celery stalks into 4-inch (10-cm) lengths. Drain the artichokes. Add the celery and artichokes to the pot, along with the 5 remaining whole carrots and the trimmed leeks. Season the broth with salt to taste. Raise the heat for a few minutes to bring back to a simmer. Cover and simmer until the vegetables and meat are tender, 20–30 minutes longer. Remove from the heat and let stand for 5–6 minutes.

🌿 Just before the meat and vegetables have finished cooking, make the green sauce and cover to keep warm. Then, to serve, transfer the meat to a serving platter and slice thinly. Remove the vegetables from the cooking liquid and place them around the meat. Spoon the warm green sauce over the meat.

SERVES 4

LAMB STEW WITH POLENTA

1½ lb (750 g) ripe plum (Roma) tomatoes
3 tablespoons olive oil
3 cloves garlic, minced (1 tablespoon)
1 small yellow onion, chopped (about ½ cup/2 oz/60 g)
2 lb (1 kg) lean, boneless lamb shoulder, cut into 1-inch (2.5-cm) cubes
   and trimmed of excess fat
½ cup (4 fl oz/125 ml) chicken broth
1 cup (5 oz/155 g) European black olives, such as Gaeta, Kalamata or
   Spanish, pitted if desired
2 lemon zest strips *(see glossary, page 126)*, each 2 inches (5 cm)
   by 1 inch (2.5 cm)
2 whole cloves
2 fresh rosemary sprigs, coarsely chopped, plus extra sprigs for garnish
Polenta with Parmesan cheese *(recipe on page 45)*
Salt and freshly ground pepper
1 teaspoon cornstarch (cornflour) mixed with 2 tablespoons water, if needed

❧ Core and peel the tomatoes (see glossary, page 124). Cut in half crosswise and squeeze out the seeds. Chop the tomatoes coarsely; set aside.

❧ In a large sauté pan over medium-low heat, warm 1 tablespoon of the oil. Add the garlic and sauté for 30–40 seconds. Add the onion and sauté until translucent, 4–5 minutes. Using a slotted spoon, transfer the onions and garlic to a plate.

❧ Add the remaining 2 tablespoons oil to the pan, raise the heat to medium-high and add half of the lamb cubes. Sauté, turning, until lightly browned on all sides, 4–6 minutes. Transfer to the plate with the onions. Repeat with the remaining lamb. Pour off any fat left in the pan.

❧ Return the meat and onions to the pan. Add the tomatoes, broth and olives. Make a bouquet garni: Place the lemon strips, whole cloves and chopped rosemary in the center of a 6-inch (15-cm) piece of cheesecloth (muslin). Gather the edges together and tie with kitchen string. Add to the pan. Cover and barely simmer over low heat, stirring occasionally, until the meat is tender, about 1½ hours. Begin to cook the polenta about 30 minutes before the stew is ready.

❧ When the stew is done, remove the bouquet garni and discard. Season to taste with salt and pepper. If a thicker stew is desired, stir in the cornstarch-water mixture. Cook over medium heat, stirring, until the sauce thickens a little.

❧ To serve, spoon the polenta onto warmed plates, then spoon the stew partially over it. Garnish each serving with a rosemary sprig. Top the polenta with a little of the Parmesan cheese, passing the remaining cheese in a bowl.

SERVES 4

NOTES

What could be more typically Italian than a simple lamb stew with tomatoes and black olives seasoned with garlic, lemon and rosemary, all served over polenta? I enjoyed just such a dish at a restaurant near Florence in the early 1970s, and I've been making my own version of it ever since.

For such a stew to be at its very best, the meat must be young lamb—boneless cubes cut from the shoulder and with all fat removed before cooking. The pieces need to be seared quickly to seal in their juices and develop their flavor, then combined with the other ingredients and slowly simmered to tenderness.

Take care, as well, to cook the polenta slowly and serve it the instant it is done.

NOTES

Baking salmon on top of Swiss chard keeps the fish moist and eases the removal of the delicate fillets from the baking dish.

Fresh cucumber relish, quickly and easily prepared, is an especially good accompaniment to the salmon. Use the freshest-looking cucumber you can find. An English hothouse cucumber would be best, as it is particularly mild and has very small seeds and a thin skin.

If fresh dill is unavailable, substitute 1 teaspoon dried dill, using your thumb to crush it in the palm of your hand to bring out the flavor and aroma. For the best results, prepare the relish an hour ahead to allow time for the flavors to develop.

BAKED SALMON ON CHARD

FOR THE CUCUMBER RELISH:
1 medium cucumber, preferably English (hothouse)
½ red bell pepper (capsicum), seeded, deribbed and cut into ¼-inch (6-mm) dice (about ½ cup/2½ oz/75 g)
2 or 3 green (spring) onions, including some tender green tops, finely chopped (about 2 tablespoons)
1 teaspoon chopped fresh dill
¼ cup (2 fl oz/60 ml) white cider vinegar
2½ tablespoons sugar
⅛ teaspoon salt

2–3 tablespoons extra-virgin olive oil
8 green Swiss chard leaves
Salt
4 salmon fillets, 6–7 oz (185–220 g) each, skin removed
Freshly ground pepper

About 1 hour before serving, make the cucumber relish: Peel the cucumber and cut in half lengthwise. Using a small spoon or melon baller, scoop out the seeds and discard. Cut the cucumber into ¼-inch (6-mm) dice; you should have about 1½ cups (7½ oz/235 g).

In a bowl, combine the cucumber, bell pepper, green onions and dill. In a separate small bowl, combine the cider vinegar, sugar and salt. Stir until the sugar and salt dissolve. Add the sweetened vinegar to the cucumber mixture and stir well. Taste and adjust the seasoning. Set aside at room temperature for 50–60 minutes, stirring frequently.

Position a rack in the middle of an oven and preheat to 425°F (220°C).

Select a baking dish that will accommodate the salmon fillets comfortably in a single layer. Brush the bottom of the dish with some of the olive oil.

Rinse the chard leaves. Trim the white stems from the chard, including the first 2 inches (5 cm) that protrude into the leaves. Discard the stems. Fold the leaves in half crosswise, sprinkle them with water and arrange in 4 stacks of 2 leaves each in the bottom of the dish. Sprinkle the chard with a little salt and lay a salmon fillet, skinned side down, on each chard stack. Brush the salmon with olive oil and sprinkle to taste with salt and pepper.

Bake, uncovered, until the salmon flesh is opaque throughout when pierced with the tip of a knife, 12–15 minutes.

Using a spatula, carefully transfer the fillets with their chard leaves to warmed plates. Top each fillet with 3–4 spoonfuls of the cucumber relish. Serve at once.

SERVES 4

SEAFOOD STEW

1 lb (500 g) ripe plum (Roma) tomatoes
2 small fennel bulbs, 1½–2 lb (750 g–1 kg) total weight, stems removed
3 tablespoons extra-virgin olive oil, plus extra for brushing on bread
3 cloves garlic, chopped (about 2 teaspoons)
2 bay leaves
1 tablespoon fresh lemon juice
1 cup (8 fl oz/250 ml) dry white wine
2 cups (16 fl oz/500 ml) bottled clam juice
4 cups (32 fl oz/1 l) water
2 teaspoons salt
Pinch of red pepper flakes
12–14 mussels in the shell, well scrubbed
2 lb (1 kg) assorted white fish such as sea bass, halibut, red snapper and sole,
  in any combination, cut into 2-inch (5-cm) pieces
½ lb (250 g) small shrimp (prawns), peeled (leave tail fin attached) and deveined
4 slices crusty country-style bread, each about ½ inch (12 mm) thick
Coarsely chopped flat-leaf (Italian) parsley for garnish

Core and peel the tomatoes (see glossary, page 124). Cut in half crosswise and squeeze out the seeds. Chop the tomatoes coarsely; set aside.

Trim the root end of each fennel bulb and remove any stalks. Cut the bulbs in half lengthwise and then cut each half lengthwise into 4 wedges; set aside.

In a large saucepan or pot over medium-low heat, warm the 3 tablespoons olive oil. Add the garlic and sauté until it just begins to change color, 1–2 minutes. Add the tomatoes, fennel and bay leaves and cook, uncovered, until the tomatoes start to release their juices, 8–10 minutes. Stir in the lemon juice, wine, clam juice, water, salt and red pepper flakes. Cover partially and cook over low heat until the fennel is almost tender, 20–25 minutes.

Meanwhile, discard any mussels that do not close to the touch; set aside.

When the fennel is almost tender, add the fish pieces, cover and barely simmer over low heat for 10 minutes. Add the mussels and shrimp and continue to barely simmer until the fish is opaque throughout when pierced with a sharp knife, the shrimp are pink and the mussels are open, another 5–6 minutes. Discard any mussels that did not open. Taste and adjust the seasoning.

Meanwhile, preheat an oven to 325°F (165°C). Brush each bread slice with oil and arrange on a baking sheet, oiled side up. Warm in the oven, a few minutes.

To serve, place a warm bread slice in each of 4 deep, warmed soup bowls. Ladle the stew over the bread and garnish with chopped parsley. Serve at once.

SERVES 4

With so many regions of Italy facing the sea, recipes for fish stew abound, each with its own distinctive personality. Arguably the two things most of these recipes have in common, however, are the presence of tomatoes and the utter simplicity of their presentation. The simple version I offer here includes fennel, which has a fresh anise flavor that naturally complements seafood. Wait until the fennel is cooked tender before you add the fish, since the latter requires just a few minutes of cooking.

Good country-style Italian or French bread is an absolute necessity for soaking up the flavorful juices.

BROILED SWORDFISH WITH GREEN OLIVES

Fish cooked or garnished with olives and oregano is a popular dish of southern Italy and most likely illustrates the influence of nearby Greece.

Fresh oregano, of course, is your best choice, but if it is unavailable, substitute 2 teaspoons of the dried herb, using your thumb to crush it in the palm of your hand to release its essential oils and thus its flavor.

Find a good brand of green olives packed in brine. Those imported from Italy, Spain or Greece will have the crispest texture and the brightest, cleanest flavor.

2 lemons
⅛ teaspoon salt
¼ cup (2 fl oz/60 ml) extra-virgin olive oil
1 tablespoon minced fresh oregano, plus 4 oregano sprigs for garnish (optional)
2 tablespoons fine fresh bread crumbs
Freshly ground pepper
4 swordfish steaks, each 6–7 oz (185–220 g) and ¾ inch (2 cm) thick
10–12 green olives in brine, preferably Italian, Greek or Spanish, pitted and thinly sliced

Using a zester or fine-holed shredder, shred the zest (yellow part only) from 1 of the lemons directly onto a small plate (see glossary, page 126). Set aside.

🌿 Squeeze the juice from the lemon into a small bowl; you should have about 2 tablespoons. Add the salt and stir to dissolve. Add the olive oil, the 1 tablespoon oregano, bread crumbs and pepper to taste. Whisk until well blended.

🌿 If there is any skin on the swordfish steaks, remove it with a sharp knife. In a glass or porcelain dish that will accommodate the steaks comfortably in a single layer, spoon in half of the lemon-oil mixture to cover the bottom. Arrange the fish steaks in the dish and spoon the other half of the lemon-oil mixture over the steaks. Marinate at room temperature for 20–25 minutes, turning over the steaks a couple of times.

🌿 Preheat a broiler (griller) with the broiling pan and rack in place. Remove the steaks from the dish, reserving the marinade, and place on the rack of the broiling pan. Place under the broiler and broil (grill) until the flesh is opaque throughout when pierced with the tip of a sharp knife, 5–6 minutes on each side, depending upon the thickness of the fish. Plan on about 10 minutes per inch (2.5 cm) at the thickest part of the fish; do not overcook.

🌿 Meanwhile, transfer the reserved marinade to a small saucepan and place over low heat until hot. Cut the remaining lemon lengthwise into quarters; set aside.

🌿 When the swordfish steaks are done, carefully transfer to warmed plates. Top with the hot marinade. Scatter the green olive slices over the fish and sprinkle with the lemon zest. Garnish with the oregano sprigs, if desired, and lemon wedges and serve immediately.

SERVES 4

HALIBUT WITH TOMATOES AND PINE NUTS

¼ cup (1½ oz/45 g) pine nuts
2 lb (1 kg) ripe plum (Roma) tomatoes
3 tablespoons olive oil, preferably a flavorful oil
3 cloves garlic, chopped (about 1 tablespoon)
1 bay leaf
2 tablespoons chopped fresh dill or 1 tablespoon dried dill
1 cup (8 fl oz/250 ml) dry white wine or water
½ teaspoon salt
Freshly ground pepper
4 halibut fillets, 6–7 oz (185–220 g) each
Coarsely chopped flat-leaf (Italian) parsley for garnish
1 lemon, cut into wedges

In a heavy frying pan over medium heat, toast the pine nuts, stirring, until lightly colored and fragrant, 1–2 minutes. Set aside.

❧ Core and peel the tomatoes (see glossary, page 124). Cut the tomatoes in half crosswise and carefully squeeze out the seeds. Chop the tomatoes coarsely; you should have 4–4½ cups (1½–1¾ lb/750–875 g).

❧ In a large sauté pan or deep frying pan over medium-low heat, warm the olive oil. Add the garlic and sauté gently, stirring, until it just starts to change color, 1–2 minutes. Add the bay leaf, dill and tomatoes and cook gently, uncovered, until the tomatoes start to break down and release their juices, 8–10 minutes. Stir in the wine or water, salt, and pepper to taste. Continue to cook, uncovered, until the tomatoes have broken down and are tender, about 10 minutes longer. Taste and adjust the seasoning; it should be highly seasoned.

❧ Carefully lay the fish fillets on top of the tomatoes in a single layer. Cover and barely simmer over low heat until the fish flesh is opaque throughout when pierced with the tip of a sharp knife, 12–15 minutes, depending upon the thickness of the fish. Plan on about 10 minutes per inch (2.5 cm) at the thickest part of the fish; do not overcook.

❧ To serve, carefully transfer the fillets to warmed plates. Spoon the tomato sauce over the top and around each fillet. Garnish with the toasted pine nuts and parsley and arrange lemon wedges alongside. Serve immediately.

SERVES 4

During summer, when tomatoes are at their best, you'll find some version of this simple fish dish in almost every restaurant in Italy. Fish and tomatoes have a strong affinity. With garlic and dill, the result is even better.

Select a particularly full-flavored, fruity extra-virgin olive oil for this dish. If you have good fresh country-style bread, place a slice on each plate to help soak up the ample juices. Other flaky white fish, such as bass, sea bass or snapper, can be substituted for the halibut.

FRESH TUNA WITH MINT AND CORIANDER

In Sicily, where tuna is a common catch, mint and coriander frequently season the fish, a sign of the culinary influence of North Africa.

Seek out only the very freshest tuna from a reputable seafood merchant. The fish should not have any strong flavor, only a fresh, clean ocean scent. Quick searing in a hot pan is all that is necessary to cook the tuna; left any longer on the heat, the fish is likely to dry out.

1 tablespoon unsalted butter
1 tablespoon olive oil
1 medium-sized sweet white onion, diced (1–1¼ cups/4–5 oz/125–155 g)
4 tuna steaks, each 6–7 oz (185–220 g) and ½ inch (12 mm) thick
Salt and freshly ground pepper
¼ cup (2 fl oz/60 ml) white wine vinegar
¼ cup (2 fl oz/60 ml) water
¼ cup chopped fresh mint, plus extra mint leaves for garnish
⅛ teaspoon ground coriander

In a large sauté pan or frying pan over medium-low heat, melt the butter with the olive oil. When hot, add the onion and sauté gently, stirring, until translucent, 8–10 minutes. Using a slotted spoon, transfer all of the onion to a plate, leaving as much of the oil in the pan as possible. Set the onion aside.

🌿 Raise the heat to high. When very hot but not smoking, add the tuna steaks and sear quickly, turning once, until lightly golden, about 2 minutes on each side. Season lightly with salt and pepper to taste and carefully transfer to a warmed serving platter or to individual warmed plates. Cover to keep warm.

🌿 Reduce the heat to medium-low. Return the onions to the pan and add the wine vinegar and water. Simmer for a few seconds, then add the chopped mint and the coriander. Simmer for a few seconds longer and season to taste with salt and pepper.

🌿 Spoon the onion mixture over the tuna steaks and garnish with the mint leaves. Serve immediately.

SERVES 4

BAKED SEA BASS IN PARCHMENT

NOTES

1½–2 lb (750 g–1 kg) sea bass fillet, in one piece, skin removed
Extra-virgin olive oil
2 or 3 large cloves garlic (depending upon your taste), thinly sliced
2–4 very small fresh rosemary sprigs (depending upon your taste),
    plus extra sprigs for garnish
Salt and freshly ground pepper
2 tablespoons capers, rinsed and drained
Chopped flat-leaf (Italian) parsley for garnish
Lemon wedges

Position a rack in the middle of an oven and preheat to 425°F (220°C). Cut a piece of parchment (baking) paper or aluminum foil that will enclose the fish fillet comfortably.

Lay the sheet of parchment or foil on a flat surface. Brush an area in the center, about the size of the fish, with olive oil. Sprinkle with half of the garlic slices and top with 1 or 2 rosemary sprigs. Lay the fish on top and brush the top of the fish with olive oil. Sprinkle with the remaining garlic slices and top with 1 or 2 rosemary sprigs. Sprinkle to taste with salt and pepper.

Enclose the fish in the parchment or foil by folding in the sides and then folding the edges together, sealing well. Place the packet on a baking sheet. Bake until the flesh is opaque throughout when pierced with the tip of a knife, 15–20 minutes, depending upon the thickness of the fish. Plan on about 10 minutes per inch (2.5 cm) at the thickest part of the fish; do not overcook. To check for doneness, open the corner of the packet and pierce the fish with the tip of a sharp knife; if not yet ready, reseal and bake a few minutes longer.

Remove the packet from the oven, then open it up and carefully transfer the fish to a warmed serving platter. Top with the capers and parsley. Arrange the lemon wedges and rosemary sprigs around the fish. Spoon the juices from the packet over the fish and serve at once.

SERVES 4

No matter where one lives in Italy, the sea is nearby, so it is only natural that Italians love fish. One of their favorite ways to prepare it is wrapped in parchment paper and baked, a method that not only yields moist, tender results, but is also quick and easy. Aluminum foil can be used in place of the parchment.

A little garlic or onion is usually tucked into the parcel along with herbs, lemon and, if the fish is not an oily variety, a little olive oil. For this recipe I've chosen sea bass, which comes out moist and flaky. You can substitute any mild-flavored, non-oily fish, such as halibut, haddock, bass, snapper, sole or turbot.

This dish is excellent served with Baked Stuffed Tomatoes with Basil (see page 99).

NOTES

Wine has been used in Italian cooking since the days of ancient Rome. One of the most popular choices of recent times is Marsala, an amber, aromatic wine used in many meat dishes and desserts, as well as with some vegetables.

Carrots and Marsala go together especially well. Rich, crunchy hazelnuts seem to add just the right finishing touch to this easy but memorable side dish.

GLAZED CARROTS WITH MARSALA AND HAZELNUTS

½ cup (2½ oz/75 g) hazelnuts (filberts)
1 lb (500 g) carrots (6 or 7)
1 cup (8 fl oz/250 ml) water
½ teaspoon salt
3 tablespoons unsalted butter
2 shallots, minced (2 tablespoons)
½ cup (4 fl oz/125 ml) dry Marsala, preferably Italian
⅓ cup (3 oz/90 g) sugar
Bouquets of fresh aromatic herbs, such as mint, rosemary, basil, oregano and dill, preferably with blossoms, for garnish

Position a rack in the middle of an oven and preheat to 325°F (165°C). Spread the hazelnuts on a baking sheet and bake until the nuts begin to change color, are fragrant and the skins split and loosen, 5–10 minutes. Let cool for a few minutes. When cool enough to handle, wrap the nuts in a clean kitchen towel and rub against them with the palms of your hands to remove most of the skins. Transfer to a coarse-mesh sieve and shake the nuts to separate them from their skins. Do not worry if small bits of the skins remain. Chop the nuts coarsely and set aside.

🐚 Peel the carrots and cut in half crosswise. Cut the upper (thicker) portions in half lengthwise so that all the pieces are more or less uniform in size (this ensures they will cook evenly and quickly). In a sauté pan or large saucepan over medium-high heat, combine the carrots, water, salt and 1 tablespoon of the butter. Bring to a boil, reduce the heat to low, cover tightly and barely simmer until the carrots are tender when pierced with the tip of a sharp knife, 10–15 minutes. If the liquid begins to cook away, add a few tablespoons water. Drain, transfer to a plate and set aside.

🐚 In the same pan over medium-low heat, melt the remaining 2 tablespoons butter. Add the shallots and sauté gently, stirring, until translucent, 4–5 minutes. Add the Marsala and sugar and simmer, stirring, until the sugar dissolves. Continue to simmer, stirring occasionally, until thickened to a medium syrup consistency, 4–5 minutes. Return the carrots to the pan, add the chopped hazelnuts and carefully turn the carrots in the syrup until well coated.

🐚 Transfer the carrots to a warmed serving dish or warmed individual plates. Spoon the glaze and hazelnuts over the carrots. Garnish with the herb bouquets and serve immediately.

SERVES 4

ITALIAN GREEN BEANS WITH MINT

For a short time every summer, markets carry green beans known as Italian or romano beans. They are wider and flatter than most common varieties, and are similar to runner beans. I find their flavor excellent, and when young (about 4 inches/10 cm long) they generally have a tender texture and cook quickly, usually in only 3–4 minutes. Be sure the beans are small and very fresh; otherwise they are not worth preparing this way.

You can, of course, make this recipe with any variety of tender, fresh young green beans, although the cooking time will be closer to 4–5 minutes. The secret to the dish is the mint, an herb that has been popular since Roman times and goes very well with other vegetables as well.

⅓ cup (2 oz/60 g) pine nuts
1 lb (500 g) young Italian green beans or other young, tender green beans
Salt
3 tablespoons olive oil
1 small sweet white onion, chopped (about ½ cup/2 oz/60 g)
2 tablespoons water
2 tablespoons chopped fresh mint
Freshly ground pepper
1 lemon

In a heavy frying pan over medium heat, toast the pine nuts, stirring, until lightly colored and fragrant, 1–2 minutes. Set aside.

🌿 Trim off the ends of the beans and cut the beans in half crosswise; each piece should be about 2 inches (5 cm) long. Fill a large saucepan three-fourths full of water and bring to a rapid boil over high heat. Add 2 teaspoons salt and the beans, quickly bring back to a boil and cook, uncovered, until the beans are just tender to the bite, 3–4 minutes. Drain immediately and plunge into cold water to stop the cooking. Set aside.

🌿 In a large sauté pan or frying pan over medium-low heat, warm the olive oil. Add the onion and sauté gently, stirring, until translucent, 4–5 minutes. Add the water, cover and cook for another 3–4 minutes; do not allow to brown.

🌿 Add the beans, mint and toasted pine nuts, raise the heat to medium-high and heat, tossing the beans gently, to serving temperature. Season to taste with salt and pepper.

🌿 Transfer to a warmed serving dish. Using a zester or a fine-holed shredder, shred the zest (yellow part only) from the lemon directly onto the beans (see glossary, page 126). Serve at once.

SERVES 4

SWISS CHARD AND POACHED EGGS WITH POLENTA

2 bunches green or red Swiss chard, about 2 lb (1 kg) total weight
Salt
¼ cup (2 fl oz/60 ml) water
Polenta with Parmesan cheese *(recipe on page 45)*
2 tablespoons cider vinegar
8 very fresh eggs
Freshly grated nutmeg
Freshly ground pepper

Rinse the chard leaves well and drain. Trim the white stems from the chard, including the first 2 inches (5 cm) that protrude into each leaf. Discard the stems. Stack the leaves in 2 piles on a cutting surface and, using a sharp knife, cut into strips 1 inch (2.5 cm) wide.

❧ Place the chard in a large sauté pan or large saucepan, sprinkle with a little salt and add the water. Cover and set aside.

❧ Begin to cook the polenta as directed. While the polenta is cooking, place the chard over medium-high heat and cook, turning it several times, until wilted and tender, about 10 minutes. Transfer to a colander and, using a spoon, press against the chard to remove all the liquid. Fluff up with a fork. Place the colander over a pan of hot water and cover to keep warm.

❧ Meanwhile, poach the eggs: Fill a large, shallow pan with warm water, cover to keep warm and set aside. In a large sauté pan or deep frying pan, pour in water to a depth of 1½ inches (4 cm). Add the vinegar and 1 teaspoon salt. Bring to a simmer over medium heat. Working in 2 or 3 batches, break the eggs, one at a time, into a saucer and, holding the saucer close to the surface of the water, slip each egg into the barely simmering water. Using a kitchen spoon, ease the whites as close to the yolks as possible. When the whites have firmed up a little, spoon the barely simmering water over the eggs and continue to cook until the whites are just set and the yolks are just glazed over but still liquid, 3–5 minutes. Using a slotted spoon or spatula, carefully transfer the eggs to the pan of warm water. Poach the remaining eggs in the same way.

❧ To serve, fluff up the chard again and divide among 4 warmed plates. Sprinkle with a little nutmeg. Using a slotted spoon, pick up 1 poached egg at a time, press a paper towel against the underside of the spoon to soak up the excess moisture and then place the egg on top of the chard, putting 2 eggs on each plate. Sprinkle the eggs with a little salt and pepper. Spoon the hot polenta onto each plate. Top the polenta with some of the remaining Parmesan cheese and serve at once. Pass the rest of the cheese in a bowl.

SERVES 4

BRAISED FENNEL IN MILK

2–3 small fennel bulbs, about 1½ lb (750 g)
¾ cup (6 fl oz/180 ml) milk
2 tablespoons unsalted butter, cut into small cubes
Salt and freshly ground pepper
¼ cup (1 oz/30 g) freshly grated Italian Parmesan cheese,
   preferably Parmigiano-Reggiano

Trim off any stems and bruised stalks from the fennel bulbs; save any feathery sprigs for garnish. Trim the root end but leave the core intact. Cut each bulb in half lengthwise and then cut each half lengthwise into 4 wedges; the portion of the core with each wedge will hold it together.

In a large sauté pan or frying pan, arrange the fennel wedges, in a single layer if possible. Add the milk, then dot the surface with the butter cubes and sprinkle with salt and pepper to taste. Bring to a simmer over medium heat, reduce the heat to medium-low, cover partially and simmer for 15 minutes; watch carefully that the milk does not boil over. Turn the wedges over once during cooking. Uncover, raise the heat slightly and cook until the fennel is just tender when pierced with a sharp knife and the milk is reduced to 1–2 tablespoons, about 15 minutes longer.

Meanwhile, position a rack in the middle of an oven and preheat to 400°F (200°C). Butter a baking dish in which the fennel wedges will fit comfortably. Using a spatula, carefully transfer the fennel, with its liquid, to the baking dish, arranging the wedges in a single layer. Top with the Parmesan cheese. Bake until golden on top, 10–15 minutes.

To serve, chop any reserved feathery sprigs and use for garnish. Serve at once.

SERVES 4

Those people who have only encountered fresh fennel as part of a salad in Italian restaurants are often surprised by how good it can be when cooked. It develops a delightful flavor, with only subtle hints of anise. In Italy, you'll find fennel grilled, fried, sautéed, roasted and prepared as a gratin. I prefer cooking the vegetable in milk, which further mellows its flavor.

Take care to cook the fennel just until tender. Any longer, and it can fall apart and lose its appeal.

Roasted red peppers like these are a classic item on menus in Italy, and for good reason. Deliciously sweet when roasted, the peppers make an excellent hot accompaniment to a main course. They can also be served cold as a first course or as part of an *antipasto* table.

Today, with air transport, red peppers are available from some part of the world year-round. But the dish is likely to be at its best, and cost the least, if you make it in summertime—when local peppers are plentiful and in peak condition.

You can prepare the peppers ahead of time, right up to their final baking. Leave them covered at room temperature for up to 2 hours before putting them in the oven.

If fresh oregano is unavailable, substitute fresh marjoram, basil, dill or mint.

ROASTED RED PEPPERS WITH OREGANO

1½–2 lb (750 g–1 kg) red bell peppers (capsicums)
3 tablespoons olive oil
2 cloves garlic, minced
1 small sweet white onion, chopped (about ½ cup/2 oz/60 g)
2 teaspoons chopped fresh oregano
2 tablespoons balsamic vinegar
Salt and freshly ground pepper
Coarsely chopped fresh flat-leaf (Italian) parsley for garnish

Roast and peel the bell peppers (see glossary, page 125). Cut the peppers lengthwise into strips ½ inch (12 mm) wide. Set aside.

❧ Position a rack in the middle of an oven and set the temperature to 375°F (190°C). In a small saucepan over medium-low heat, warm 1 tablespoon of the olive oil. When hot, add the garlic and sauté gently, stirring, for 30–40 seconds. Add the onion and sauté slowly, stirring, until the onion is translucent, 4–5 minutes; do not allow to brown. Remove from the heat, add the oregano and stir to blend. Transfer to a rectangular or oval baking dish, spreading the mixture evenly over the bottom. Arrange the peppers evenly in the dish.

❧ In a small bowl, combine the balsamic vinegar and a little salt and pepper. Using a small whisk, stir until well blended, then whisk in the remaining 2 tablespoons olive oil. Spoon evenly over the peppers. Cover the dish with aluminum foil and bake for 10 minutes. Remove the foil and continue to bake until the peppers are very tender, another 5–10 minutes.

❧ Garnish with the parsley and serve immediately.

SERVES 4

MASHED POTATOES WITH ROSEMARY AND LEMON

2 lb (1 kg) Alaska (Yukon) Gold or Finnish Yellow potatoes
3 fresh rosemary sprigs, plus extra for garnish
Salt
1 tablespoon mild extra-virgin olive oil
1 cup (8 fl oz/250 ml) milk, heated
Freshly ground pepper
1 lemon

If you will be mashing the potatoes with a ricer, simply cut them into 1–1½-inch (2.5–4-cm) pieces. If you will be using a food mill or a hand masher, first peel the potatoes and then cut into 1–1½-inch (2.5–4-cm) pieces.

❧ Place the potatoes in a saucepan and add water to cover by 1 inch (2.5 cm). Place the 3 rosemary sprigs in a square of cheesecloth (muslin), gather the edges together to form a sachet and tie with kitchen string. Add to the pan along with 1 tablespoon salt. Place over medium-high heat and bring to a boil. Reduce the heat slightly, cover partially and gently boil until the potatoes are just tender when pierced with the tip of a sharp knife, 15–20 minutes.

❧ Remove the rosemary and discard. Drain the potatoes. Place the potatoes in a potato ricer held over the saucepan and push the handle to purée. Alternatively, after draining, return the potatoes to the saucepan and mash them with a potato masher until they are free of lumps. Or you can purée the potatoes using a food mill fitted with the fine disk.

❧ Return the saucepan to very low heat, add the olive oil and beat vigorously with a wooden spoon until well blended. Add the warm milk, a little at a time, continuing to beat and scraping the sides and bottom of the pan each time, until the potatoes are smooth and fluffy. You may not need all of the milk to achieve the correct consistency. Add salt and pepper to taste and continue to stir over low heat until very hot.

❧ Spoon the potatoes into a warmed serving dish. Using a zester or fine-holed shredder, shred the zest (yellow part only) from the lemon directly onto the potatoes (see glossary, page 126). Garnish with fresh rosemary and serve immediately.

SERVES 4

NOTES

If you've ever eaten mashed or puréed potatoes in Italy or France, you'll probably understand why I specify Alaska Gold or Finnish Yellow potatoes—varieties that are similar to those used by Italian and French cooks. These small, waxy, golden potatoes can be mashed or puréed smoothly and quickly, producing results that are superior in flavor and consistency to most other potatoes. If you can't find them, use russet or other waxy boiling potatoes. I find that red new potatoes are not the best choice for mashed potatoes.

A potato ricer (see page 121) is the easiest and most efficient way to mash potatoes. The pulp is easily forced through the small holes to produce a fine texture. And a ricer also eliminates the need to peel the potatoes—a real time-saver—as the skins remain in the ricer when the pulp is forced through.

SAUTÉED ZUCCHINI AND MUSHROOMS

Often referred to as Italian squash, zucchini have invaded the world's food markets and home gardens, probably because they are incredibly easy to grow, are prolific in their yield and are highly versatile in the kitchen. The Italians, certainly, make good and frequent use of them in their cuisine.

The vegetables you select for this recipe must be young and fresh. The mushrooms, in particular, should be small and very firm, with no brown gills showing beneath their caps.

The zest of the lemon brings out the flavors of the vegetables and herbs. Have everything else ready to serve before you begin cooking this dish, so that the zucchini and mushrooms arrive at the table hot and crisp.

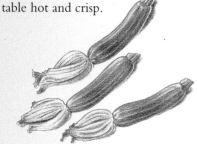

1 lb (500 g) small zucchini (courgettes)
Salt
1 lb (500 g) small, firm fresh mushrooms
5 tablespoons (3 fl oz/80 ml) olive oil
2 cloves garlic, chopped
¼ cup firmly packed, finely shredded fresh basil leaves
Freshly ground pepper
1 lemon

Trim off the ends of the zucchini and cut on the diagonal into slices ½ inch (12 mm) thick. Place in a colander and sprinkle with salt, tossing to distribute the salt evenly. Spread the zucchini out in the colander. Let stand over a bowl or in the sink for 40–50 minutes to drain off excess moisture and bitterness. Rinse and pat dry with a clean kitchen towel. Set aside.

Using a soft brush or a clean kitchen towel, clean the mushrooms of any bits of soil; do not wash. Trim the stems. Cut the mushrooms into slices ¼ inch (6 mm) thick. Place in a bowl and set aside.

In a large sauté pan or frying pan over medium heat, warm 2 tablespoons of the olive oil. Add the zucchini and sauté, tossing often, until tender but still firm, 8–10 minutes. Transfer to a bowl and set aside.

Add another 2 tablespoons olive oil to the same pan over medium-high heat. Add the mushrooms and sauté, tossing often, until the mushrooms begin to soften, 6–7 minutes. Transfer to the bowl with the zucchini.

Add the remaining 1 tablespoon olive oil to the pan, reduce the heat to medium-low and add the garlic. Sauté gently, stirring, until the garlic just begins to change color, 30–40 seconds.

Return the mushrooms and zucchini to the pan and add the basil and salt and pepper to taste. Raise the heat and toss until the vegetables are hot.

Transfer to a warmed serving dish. Using a zester or fine-holed shredder, shred the zest (yellow part only) from the lemon directly onto the vegetables (see glossary, page 126). Serve immediately.

SERVES 4

BAKED STUFFED TOMATOES WITH BASIL

3–4 slices crusty country-style Italian or French bread, preferably day-old
4 large, firm but ripe tomatoes, about ¾ lb (375 g) each
¼ cup (2 fl oz/60 ml) extra-virgin olive oil
2–3 cloves garlic (depending upon your taste), minced
¼ cup chopped fresh basil
2 tablespoons chopped fresh flat-leaf (Italian) parsley
Salt and freshly ground pepper
¼ cup (1½ oz/45 g) pine nuts

Position a rack in the middle of an oven and preheat to 400°F (200°C).

🌿 Tear the bread slices into small pieces and place in a food processor fitted with the metal blade or in a blender. Process to form fine crumbs. Measure out 2 cups (4 oz/125 g) and set aside.

🌿 Cut off the top one-fourth of the stem end of each tomato so that the seed cavities are exposed. Using a very small spoon (such as a coffee spoon), scoop out all of the seeds and liquid from each cavity; do not break down the flesh dividing the seed cavities. Sprinkle the inside of the tomatoes with salt and turn upside down in a colander or on a rack. Let stand for 30 minutes to drain off some of their liquid.

🌿 In a frying pan over medium-low heat, warm the olive oil. Add the garlic and sauté gently, stirring, for 30–40 seconds. Remove from the heat and stir in the basil and parsley. Then add the bread crumbs, stirring until well mixed. Season to taste with salt and pepper and stir again.

🌿 Spoon the bread crumb mixture into the tomatoes, filling each cavity full and mounding the filling slightly on top. Spread the leftover mixture in the bottom of a small baking dish in which the tomatoes will fit comfortably. Place the tomatoes upright in the dish and sprinkle the pine nuts evenly over them. Bake until the tomatoes are light golden on top, tender and cooked through, 30–45 minutes; the time will depend upon the ripeness of the tomatoes.

🌿 Transfer the tomatoes to warmed plates. Spoon the bread crumb mixture from the baking dish alongside. Serve immediately.

SERVES 4

NOTES

The success of this recipe depends entirely upon finding firm, flavorful, vine-ripened tomatoes, so it is advisable to make it only at the height of summer. You will also need fresh basil, which is most plentiful and inexpensive at that time of year.

Choose tomatoes that are more or less the same size and shape, being sure they sit upright in the dish.

Although the tomatoes must be baked until they are very tender, be careful not to overcook them or they will become mushy. If you like, mix a little freshly grated Parmesan cheese with the bread crumbs.

Italy's popular flat bread, focaccia, is another of the country's culinary treasures that is gaining permanent popularity abroad—and for good reason. Tasty and easy to prepare, it is, in simplest terms, nothing more than a pizza without the topping.

This version includes fresh rosemary, a little sugar, olive oil and white grapes to produce a marvelously light, mild, sweet bread. Serve it warm with coffee on a Sunday morning, with tea in the afternoon, or for a lunch dessert. It is a delightful substitute for coffee cake or Danish pastry.

Please take a look at the suggestions about working with yeast and mixing and rising dough in the note on page 102 and on page 124.

GRAPE FOCACCIA

Focaccia dough *(recipe on page 118)*
2 tablespoons sugar

FOR THE GRAPE TOPPING:
3 tablespoons extra-virgin olive oil
4 fresh rosemary sprigs
1½ cups (9 oz/280 g) ripe seedless white grapes, rinsed and dried
¼ cup (2 oz/60 g) sugar

Make the focaccia dough as directed, adding the 2 tablespoons sugar with the salt and reducing the olive oil in the bread to 1 tablespoon.

While the dough is rising, begin to make the topping: In a small saucepan over low heat, warm the 3 tablespoons olive oil until hot. Add 2 of the rosemary sprigs, pushing down on them to submerge completely, and set aside for the oil to absorb the rosemary flavor.

Prepare a baking pan as directed in the focaccia recipe, line it with the dough and let rise as directed. Preheat the oven as directed.

Remove the rosemary sprigs from the oil and discard. Brush the risen dough generously with the rosemary-flavored oil. Scatter the grapes evenly over the surface and carefully push each one into the dough. Sprinkle the sugar evenly over the surface. Remove the leaves from the 2 remaining rosemary sprigs (about 2 teaspoons). Leave them whole or chop them; then sprinkle them over the surface.

Bake until golden brown, 30–40 minutes. Transfer the pan to a rack and let cool for a few minutes.

Cut into squares and serve warm, preferably, or at room temperature. To reheat, place in a preheated 350°F (180°C) oven for 3–4 minutes.

MAKES ONE 10-BY-15-INCH (25-BY-37.5-CM) SHEET; SERVES 6–8

POLENTA BREAD

3 cups (15 oz/470 g) unbleached bread flour
½ cup (2½ oz/75 g) finely ground, quick-cooking Italian polenta,
  plus extra for baking sheet
2 teaspoons quick-rise yeast
1 teaspoon salt
1⅓ cups (11 fl oz/330 ml) warm tap water (110°F/43°C)
1 tablespoon extra-virgin olive oil
1 egg beaten with 1 tablespoon water

If you have found bread making intimidating or too much work, try baking this simple loaf. I think you will change your mind. It is a delicious, richly textured bread. You'll especially like it warm or toasted, at breakfast time or with soups, salads, meats or seafoods.

Purchase one of the fast-acting dry yeasts now sold in most food stores. They are much stronger and quicker than conventional active dry yeast; under ideal conditions, rising time can be shortened to less than an hour.

I have found that when you are ready to put the dough in a bowl to rise, it is a good idea to warm the bowl first with warm to moderately hot tap water; then dry the bowl, brush lightly with oil, add the dough and cover. The warmth of the bowl starts the dough rising much faster, decreasing total rising time.

If you have one, an electric mixer fitted with a dough hook can also be used to knead the dough.

In a large bowl, combine the flour, the ½ cup (2½ oz/75 g) polenta, the yeast and salt. Using a wooden spoon, stir to mix well. Add the warm water and olive oil and stir until all of the flour has been absorbed and a dough has formed.

❧ Using your hands, gather the dough into a ball and transfer to a well-floured work surface. Knead until soft and elastic and no longer sticky, about 10 minutes. Work more flour into the dough if needed to reduce stickiness; be sure to keep the work surface well floured. The dough should remain in a rounded shape and not flatten out when left on a work surface for a minute or two. If not, work a little more flour into the dough. Place the dough in a warmed, lightly oiled bowl, turning several times to coat it with oil. Cover with plastic wrap and let rise in a warm place until doubled in bulk, 45–75 minutes.

❧ Sprinkle a little polenta on a baking sheet and set aside. Punch down the dough, return to the lightly floured work surface and knead a few times. Form into a round ball or an oval shape and place on the prepared baking sheet. The dough should retain its shape and not flatten out. Cover loosely with plastic wrap and let rise in a warm place until doubled in bulk, 30–40 minutes.

❧ While the dough is rising, position a rack in the middle of an oven and preheat to 425°F (220°C).

❧ When the dough has risen, using a very sharp, thin-bladed knife or single-edge razor blade, carefully make a slash ½ inch (12 mm) deep across the top. Brush the surface with the egg mixture. Bake for 15 minutes. Reduce the temperature to 375°F (190°C); continue to bake until golden and crusty, 30–35 minutes longer.

❧ Transfer the loaf to a wire rack and let cool.

MAKES 1 ROUND OR OVAL LOAF

WALNUT RING LOAF

2 cups (10 oz/315 g) whole-wheat (wholemeal) bread flour
1 cup (5 oz/155 g) unbleached bread flour
2 teaspoons quick-rise yeast
2 teaspoons salt
1 cup (8 fl oz/250 ml) warm tap water (110°F/43°C)
1 tablespoon extra-virgin olive oil
2 tablespoons honey
½ cup (2 oz/60 g) walnut pieces, plus 10 walnut halves
1 egg beaten with 1 teaspoon water

In a large bowl, combine both flours, the yeast and salt. Using a wooden spoon, stir to mix well. Add the warm water, olive oil and honey and stir until all of the flour has been absorbed and a dough forms. Gather the dough into a ball and transfer to a well-floured work surface. Knead until soft and smooth and no longer sticky, about 10 minutes. Work in more bread flour if needed to reduce stickiness. Place in a warmed, lightly oiled bowl, turning several times to coat it with oil. Cover with plastic wrap and let rise in a warm place until doubled in bulk, 45–75 minutes.

🌿 Meanwhile, position a rack in the middle of an oven and preheat to 325°F (165°C). Spread the ½ cup (2 oz/60 g) walnut pieces on a baking sheet and bake until the nuts begin to change color, about 10 minutes. Let cool.

🌿 Oil an 8-inch (20-cm) round cake pan with 1½-inch (4-cm) sides, or a baking sheet. Punch down the dough and turn out onto a well-floured surface; knead a couple of times. Using your palms, form the dough into a log 10 inches (25 cm) long. Cut crosswise into 10 equal pieces and let rest for 5 minutes. Flatten each piece into a 3-inch (7.5-cm) round. Place a few toasted walnut pieces in the center of each round. Gather the edges of each round and pinch together to form a ball. Place the balls, seam side down and touching one another, around the perimeter of the cake pan, or on the baking sheet in a circle 8 inches (20 cm) in diameter. Cover loosely with plastic wrap and let rise in a warm place until doubled in bulk, 30–45 minutes. While the dough is rising, reposition the rack to the lower part of the oven and preheat to 375°F (190°C).

🌿 When the buns have risen, brush them with the egg mixture; do not let it run onto the pan or the buns may stick. Place a walnut half on each ball and press slightly to anchor firmly. Bake for 15 minutes, then reduce the heat to 350°F (180°C). Cover loosely with aluminum foil to keep the nuts from burning and continue to bake until golden, 20–25 minutes longer.

🌿 Immediately unmold onto a rack. Serve warm, preferably, or at room temperature. Place on a serving plate and let guests pull apart.

MAKES 1 RING LOAF

NOTES

When Williams-Sonoma opened the first Il Fornaio bakery in San Francisco in 1980, I learned to make this fragrant, flavorful loaf from one of the bakers we brought over from Italy.

I have explained making the bread by hand, but the dough can also be made in an electric mixer equipped with a dough hook. Knead at medium-low speed for about 10 minutes. And please take a look at the suggestions about working with yeast and mixing and rising dough in the note on page 102 and on page 124.

You can also bake this bread in an 8-inch (20-cm) ring mold.

APPLE WALNUT CAKE

With most Italian dessert baking done in small bakeries, it is only natural that any baking done at home would be simple and easy. This is one of the easiest, and probably the best, Italian home-baked desserts. I have added walnuts and golden raisins to the traditional recipe for more crunch and flavor. Apples that are especially sweet and hold their shape well during baking are preferable; Golden Delicious, Fuji and Gala are among the best.

If you use one of the newer springform pans with a black or dark-gray stick-resistant finish, it's a good idea to reduce your oven temperature to 325°F (165°C). Otherwise the dark finish will cause the cake to brown too quickly on the bottom and sides. I also suggest placing a baking sheet on the shelf below to catch any drips or runovers.

Serve the cake with zabaglione (see page 117) or with whipped cream flavored with lemon juice or vanilla extract.

1 lemon
4 medium-sized juicy, sweet apples, such as Golden Delicious, Fuji or Gala
1½ cups (6 oz/185 g) cake (soft-wheat) flour
1½ teaspoons baking powder
¼ teaspoon salt
½ cup (4 oz/125 g) unsalted butter
1 cup (8 oz/240 g) sugar, plus extra for sprinkling on top
3 eggs
1 teaspoon vanilla extract (essence)
½ cup (3 oz/90 g) golden raisins (sultanas), softened in boiling water to cover for 8–10 minutes and drained
½ cup (2 oz/60 g) walnuts, coarsely chopped
½ teaspoon ground cinnamon

Position a rack in the middle of an oven and preheat to 350°F (180°C). Butter and flour a 9-inch (23-cm) springform pan; it should be 2¾ inches (7 cm) deep, measured from the inside.

❧ Using a zester or fine-holed shredder, shred the zest (yellow part only) from the lemon directly into a large bowl (see glossary, page 126). Then squeeze the juice from the lemon into the bowl.

❧ Peel the apples and cut into quarters. Remove the cores and cut each quarter into thin slices. Place in the bowl with the lemon juice and toss carefully to coat all cut surfaces to prevent them from darkening. Set aside.

❧ In a separate bowl, sift together the flour, baking powder and salt. Set aside.

❧ In a bowl, using an electric mixer set at medium speed, beat the butter until light, about 2 minutes. Add ¾ cup (6 oz/180 g) of the sugar and beat until fluffy, 4–5 minutes, scraping down the bowl at intervals. Add the eggs, one at a time, beating well after each addition. Continue beating until doubled in volume, 5–6 minutes, scraping down the bowl at intervals. Beat in the vanilla. Using a rubber spatula, fold in the flour mixture, one-third at a time, until just incorporated. Pour the batter into the pan; level the surface with the spatula. Set aside.

❧ Add the raisins and walnuts to the apples and toss well. In a small bowl, stir together the remaining ¼ cup (2 oz/60 g) sugar and the cinnamon. Sprinkle over the apples and toss again. Spoon the apples evenly over the batter and then sprinkle with 1 or more tablespoons sugar. Bake until golden brown and a toothpick inserted into the center comes out clean, 50–60 minutes.

❧ Transfer the pan to a cooling rack and let rest for 8–10 minutes. Run a knife around the pan to loosen the cake. Release the pan sides and remove. Run a knife between the bottom of the cake and pan bottom and, using a metal spatula, transfer to a serving plate. Let cool to warm, then slice and serve.

SERVES 8–10

ORANGES WITH MINT AND TOASTED ALMONDS

¾ cup (3 oz/90 g) sliced (flaked) almonds, preferably blanched
6 navel oranges
1 cup (8 fl oz/250 ml) water
1 cup (8 oz/250 g) sugar
3 or 4 large fresh mint sprigs, plus mint leaves for garnish

Position a rack in the middle of an oven and preheat to 300°F (150°C). Spread the almonds on a baking sheet and bake until the nuts begin to change color and are fragrant, 4–5 minutes; do not allow to brown too much. Remove from the oven and let cool.

❧ Using a sharp paring knife, peel off the zest (orange part only) of the skin of 2 of the oranges, removing it in long pieces (see glossary, page 126). Slice the zest into strips ⅛ inch (3 mm) wide and about 2 inches (5 cm) long. Fill a saucepan half full of water and bring to a boil over medium-high heat. Add the orange zest strips, reduce the heat to medium-low and simmer, uncovered, for 15 minutes, to remove most of the bitterness. Drain and set aside.

❧ In a saucepan over medium-high heat, combine the water and sugar. Bring to a boil, stirring to dissolve the sugar. Using a brush moistened with water, brush down the pan sides to remove any sugar crystals. Reduce the heat to low, add the 3 or 4 mint sprigs and simmer until the syrup is nicely mint-flavored, 5–6 minutes. Remove the mint sprigs and discard.

❧ Add the reserved orange zest strips and simmer over medium-low heat until the syrup has thickened and the zest is translucent, 12–15 minutes. Brush down the pan sides again if you see any sugar crystals forming. Set aside to cool.

❧ Cut off a thick slice from the top and bottom of the 2 partially peeled oranges, exposing the fruit beneath the peel. Then do the same to the 4 remaining oranges. Working with 1 orange at a time, place upright on a cutting surface and, holding the orange firmly, slice off the peel in strips, cutting off the pith and membrane with it to reveal the fruit beneath. Cut the orange in half crosswise and place in a bowl. When all the oranges have been peeled and cut, cover and refrigerate until chilled.

❧ To serve, place 2 or 3 orange halves on dessert plates. Spoon the syrup and orange strips over the orange halves and sprinkle generously with the toasted almonds. Garnish with the fresh mint leaves and serve at once.

SERVES 4

NOTES

In Italy oranges are served for dessert almost everywhere, as they are especially refreshing after nearly any main course. Their preparation, however, varies from region to region. This bright, mint-scented version recalls an orange dessert made in Venice.

Navel oranges are an excellent choice here; they have a sweet, full flavor and are seedless. You may find the oranges easiest to eat with a dessert knife and fork. If you prefer, cut the fruit crosswise into thick slices.

NOTES

These Tuscan almond cookies have won worldwide popularity. In keeping with tradition, serve them with a glass of dessert wine, such as Tuscany's Vin Santo. The cookies are also excellent served with any fruit dessert, a pudding or, of course, with coffee or tea.

For the second baking, you may want to use two baking sheets so that you can spread the slices out for more uniform baking and greater crunchiness. I find that the cookies also cool better—to an even crispness—if left in the turned-off oven with the door ajar about 2 inches (5 cm).

ALMOND BISCOTTI

1 cup (5½ oz/170 g) almonds
2 cups (10 oz/315 g) all-purpose (plain) flour
1½ teaspoons baking powder
⅛ teaspoon salt
⅛ teaspoon ground cinnamon
1 teaspoon aniseeds, lightly crushed
1 small orange
¼ cup (2 oz/60 g) unsalted butter
½ cup (4 oz/125 g) granulated sugar
¼ cup (2 oz/60 g) firmly packed light brown sugar
2 eggs
2 teaspoons almond extract (essence)
½ cup (3 oz/90 g) golden raisins (sultanas)
1 egg beaten with 1 tablespoon water

Position a rack in the middle of an oven and preheat to 325°F (165°C). Spread the almonds on a baking sheet and bake until well toasted, about 10 minutes; let cool. Chop very coarsely and set aside. Raise the oven temperature to 350°F (180°C). Butter and flour a baking sheet.

In a bowl, combine the flour, baking powder, salt, cinnamon and aniseeds and stir well; set aside. Using a fine-holed grater and holding the orange over a saucer, grate the zest (orange part only) from the orange (see glossary, page 126). You should have about 1 tablespoon zest. Set aside.

In a bowl, using an electric mixer set on medium speed, beat together the butter and both sugars until light, about 5 minutes, scraping down the bowl at intervals. Add the eggs, one at a time, beating well after each addition. Beat in the almond extract and the orange zest. Reduce the speed to low and gradually beat in the flour mixture until blended. The dough should be stiff. Add the almonds and raisins and knead in with your hands. Gather into a ball, transfer to a well-floured surface and knead a few times, adding a little flour if too sticky.

Divide the dough in half. Form each half into a flattened log about 2 inches (5 cm) wide and 10 inches (25 cm) long. Place on the baking sheet, spacing them 1 inch (2.5 cm) apart. Brush the tops with the egg mixture. Bake until lightly browned, 20–25 minutes. Place the sheet on a rack to cool for 5 minutes.

Transfer the logs to a work surface. Using a sharp serrated knife, cut on the diagonal into slices 1 inch (2.5 cm) wide. Place the slices upright on the baking sheet (or 2 sheets), spacing them 1 inch (2.5 cm) apart. Return to the oven and bake until golden brown, about 15 minutes. Turn off the oven, prop open the oven door about 2 inches (5 cm) and let cool for 30–35 minutes. Transfer the baking sheet(s) to a wire rack(s) and let cool completely until dry and crisp.

MAKES 18–20

Lemon Rice Pudding with Hazelnut Meringues

Notes

The typical Italian dessert pudding, or *budino,* is baked. I chose to depart from tradition by leaving out the egg whites and cooking the pudding on the stove top. I then serve it slightly warm or at room temperature, accompanied by crisp hazelnut meringues made with the egg whites.

I think you'll find this rice pudding particularly delicious and quite different from any others. Arborio rice gives it a rich, creamy character that is lightened by the lemon. The hazelnut meringues are addictive; you will not have to store them for very long. They are excellent with coffee or tea. The recipe calls for baking and drying the meringues longer than most recipes, to give them better flavor and color.

Hazelnut meringues *(recipe on page 119)*
⅓ cup (2 oz/60 g) golden raisins (sultanas)
Boiling water, as needed
3 cups (24 fl oz/750 ml) milk
Pinch of salt
⅓ cup (2½ oz/75 g) Italian Arborio rice or medium-grain white rice
2 lemons
4 egg yolks
¼ cup (2 oz/60 g) sugar
⅛ teaspoon ground cinnamon

Make the hazelnut meringues as directed and let cool for a couple of hours.

🌿 In a small bowl, combine the raisins and boiling water to cover. Let stand for 8–10 minutes to soften. Drain well and set aside.

🌿 In a heavy-bottomed saucepan over medium heat, combine the milk and salt. Heat until small bubbles appear around the edges of the pan; watch carefully that it does not boil. Add the rice in a slow, steady stream, stirring constantly to keep the grains separate. Reduce the heat to low, cover partially and barely simmer, stirring every few minutes, until the rice is tender and the milk is creamy and thickened, 30–40 minutes; watch carefully that the milk does not boil over. Remove from the heat and let cool for 5 minutes.

🌿 Meanwhile, using a fine-holed grater, grate the zest (yellow part only) from 1 of the lemons directly onto a saucer (see glossary, page 126); be sure to scrape off all the zest clinging to the grater. You should have about 1 teaspoon zest. Set aside.

🌿 In a medium-sized heatproof bowl (or in the top pan of a double boiler), combine the egg yolks and sugar and, using a whisk, beat until light colored and creamy, 2–3 minutes. Beat in the lemon zest and the cinnamon. Using a wooden spoon, stir in the hot rice-milk mixture, a little at a time, until well blended. Stir in the raisins. Place the bowl over a pan of simmering water; do not allow the bottom to touch the water. Stir slowly, scraping the bottom and sides each time, until the mixture thickens and is creamy, 10–15 minutes. It should thickly coat the spoon. Do not allow to boil. Set aside to cool.

🌿 When cooled to warm, transfer the pudding to a serving dish. Using a zester or a fine-holed shredder, shred the zest (yellow part only) from the remaining lemon directly onto the top of the pudding.

🌿 Serve the pudding, preferably warm, with 4 or 5 hazelnut meringues alongside each serving. Pass extra meringues on a serving plate.

Serves 4–6

PINK GRAPEFRUIT GRANITA

NOTES

I think Italy has developed some of the world's best frozen desserts, and high among these I would rank granitas—confections of coarse crystals of flavored ice.

To achieve the appropriate consistency, granitas are made in the freezer compartment of a refrigerator rather than in an ice cream maker. All you have to do is take the container out of the freezer every 15–20 minutes to stir up the crystals. Use a shallow stainless-steel bowl, which freezes quickly. And make the granita the same day you plan to serve it; if stored longer it will form a solid mass.

For superior color and flavor, I use Texas Ruby grapefruit, which has a deep pink hue and a full, sweet flavor. But you could substitute any pink variety you like.

6 or 7 medium-sized pink grapefruits, preferably Texas Ruby
½ cup (4 fl oz/125 ml) water
1 cup (8 oz/250 g) sugar
2 fresh mint sprigs, or as needed, plus extra sprigs for garnish
Orange zest strips *(see glossary, page 126)* for garnish (optional)

Be sure your freezer is set at its coldest setting an hour before you begin to make the granita. Squeeze the juice from the grapefruit and strain through a fine-mesh strainer into a bowl to produce a clear juice. You will need 3–3½ cups (24–28 fl oz/750–875 ml). Cover and refrigerate until well chilled.

🌸 In a saucepan over medium heat, combine the water and sugar. Bring to a boil, stirring to dissolve the sugar. Using a brush moistened with water, brush down the pan sides to remove any sugar crystals. Add the 2 mint sprigs and boil for 1 minute. Set aside until cool enough to taste, 5–10 minutes, then taste for flavor. If the syrup has a good mint flavor, remove and discard the mint; if not, add more mint and repeat boiling and cooling. Set aside to cool completely.

🌸 When the syrup has cooled, stir it into the chilled grapefruit juice until completely blended. Pour this mixture into a shallow stainless-steel bowl or other stainless-steel container. (Ice-cube trays will work if you have nothing else at hand.) Place in the freezer.

🌸 After about 20 minutes, check to see if any ice crystals have formed. If they have, stir to break them up with a fork. Continue to check every 15–20 minutes and stir as necessary to prevent the crystals from forming a solid mass. Frequent stirring is important to producing a uniformly textured granita. Be sure to scrape any frozen crystals from the sides and bottom of the container and break them up each time. Under proper conditions, the granita should freeze in 1½–2 hours. However, if your freezer is not cold enough or too full of food, it can take up to 2–3 hours; the timing will depend upon the freezer.

🌸 To serve, place 4–6 footed glass goblets in the refrigerator 10–15 minutes before serving. Spoon the granita into the chilled goblets. Garnish with mint sprigs and orange zest strips, if desired. Serve immediately.

SERVES 4–6

MIXED BERRIES WITH ZABAGLIONE

6 cups (1½ lb/750 g) assorted ripe berries such as strawberries, raspberries, blackberries and blueberries, in any combination
¾ cup (6 fl oz/185 ml) dry white wine
3 tablespoons sugar, plus ⅓ cup (3 oz/90 g) sugar
1 lemon
4 egg yolks
½ cup (4 fl oz/125 ml) heavy (double) cream
Ground cinnamon
Fresh mint leaves for garnish

If using strawberries, remove the stems and cut in half lengthwise or, if large, cut into quarters. Place all of the berries in a bowl and toss to mix. Sprinkle with ¼ cup (2 fl oz/60 ml) of the wine and then with the 3 tablespoons sugar. Cover and refrigerate until chilled, about 1 hour, tossing carefully every 20–25 minutes.

❧ Using a fine-holed grater and holding the lemon over a saucer, grate the zest (yellow part only) from the lemon (see glossary, page 126); be sure to scrape off all the zest clinging to the grater. You should have 1 teaspoon. Set aside. Have ready a large bowl of ice cubes with a little water added.

❧ In a medium-sized heatproof bowl (or in the top pan of a double boiler), combine the egg yolks and the ⅓ cup (3 oz/90 g) sugar. Using a whisk, beat until light colored and creamy, 2–3 minutes. Add the remaining ½ cup (4 fl oz/ 125 ml) wine and whisk until well blended. Place the bowl over a pan of simmering water; do not allow the bottom to touch the water. Whisk continuously, scraping the bottom and sides of the bowl each time, until the mixture has tripled in volume and is quite thick and creamy; the top should stand in soft folds. This will take 10–15 minutes; be careful that the mixture does not get too hot or it will curdle.

❧ Quickly nest the bowl in the bowl of ice and continue to whisk until the mixture is cold; be sure to scrape the bottom and sides often, as the mixture thickens when in contact with the cold surface of the bowl. This will take 15–25 minutes; the mixture should be very thick.

❧ In a separate bowl, using a clean whisk or an electric beater, whip the cream until stiff peaks form. Stir in the lemon zest. Then, using a rubber spatula, fold the cream into the egg mixture until thoroughly combined. Use immediately, or cover and refrigerate for 2–3 hours; stir well before serving.

❧ Spoon the berries into bowls and top generously with the zabaglione. Sprinkle a little cinnamon on top and garnish with mint leaves. Any leftover zabaglione can be covered and refrigerated overnight, then whisked briefly to recombine.

SERVES 4

NOTES

The combination of summer's best berries and a topping of smooth, creamy zabaglione—a cooked, whipped froth of egg, sugar and wine blended with whipped cream—is something to look forward to on a warm summer evening. I like to make this with an assortment of berries, to get a good balance of flavor and color.

This version of zabaglione, a cousin to the traditional one made with Marsala and served warm, uses dry white wine and is whisked over ice until cool. (Save the 4 egg whites left over from this recipe to make the Hazelnut Meringues on page 119.) Lemon-flavored whipped cream is then folded in. A dash or two of cinnamon adds a touch of spice to each serving.

You can make the zabaglione topping an hour or two ahead of time and refrigerate it. Stir well before spooning it over the berries.

117

Basic Recipes

Six fundamental Italian recipes referred to through-out this book.

Focaccia

3¼ cups (16½ oz/515 g)
   unbleached bread flour
2 teaspoons quick-rise yeast
1 teaspoon salt
3 tablespoons extra-virgin
   olive oil, plus extra for
   brushing
1¼ cups (10 fl oz/310 ml)
   warm water (110°F/43°C),
   or as needed
Coarse sea salt, optional

In a large bowl, combine the flour, yeast and salt. Using a wooden spoon, stir to mix well. Add the 3 tablespoons olive oil. Then, while stirring, gradually add the 1¼ cups (10 fl oz/310 ml) warm water until all of the flour has been absorbed and a dough forms. You may not need all of the water or you may need a bit more. ❧ Using your hands, gather the dough into a ball and transfer to a well-floured work surface. Knead until soft and elastic and no longer sticky, about 10 minutes. Work more flour into the dough if needed to reduce stickiness; be sure to keep the work surface well floured. Place the dough in a warmed, lightly oiled bowl, turning several times to coat it with oil. Cover with plastic wrap and let rise in a warm place until doubled in bulk, 45–75 minutes. ❧ Position a rack in the lower part of an oven and preheat to 400°F (200°C). Brush a 10-by-15-inch (25-by-37.5-cm) baking pan with ½-inch (12-mm) sides with olive oil and set aside. ❧ Punch down the dough and transfer to the floured surface. Knead a few times, then let rest for 5–6 minutes. With the palms of your hands, form into a rectangle about 4 by 8 inches (10 by 20 cm). Roll out the dough to fit the prepared pan. Transfer the dough to the pan. Stretch and pat the dough to cover the pan bottom completely with an even thickness. Cover with plastic wrap; let rise until about 1 inch (2.5 cm) high, 20–30 minutes. ❧ Using your fingertips, make "dimple" indentations in the dough, spacing them 2 inches (5 cm) apart. Brush the surface with olive oil and sprinkle lightly with coarse sea salt, if desired. ❧ Bake until golden brown, 30–40 minutes. Transfer to a rack and let cool in the pan for a few minutes. ❧ Cut into squares and serve warm, preferably, or at room temperature. To reheat, place in a preheated 300°F (150°C) oven for 6–8 minutes.

Makes one 10-by-15-inch (25-by-37.5-cm) sheet; serves 6–8

Cannellini Beans

2 cups (14 oz/440 g) dried cannellini beans
4 cups (32 fl oz/1 l) hot tap water
1 bay leaf
2 orange zest strips *(see glossary, page 126),* each about 2 inches
   (5 cm) by 1 inch (2.5 cm) and stuck with 2 cloves
3 fresh flat-leaf (Italian) parsley sprigs
2 teaspoons salt
Freshly ground pepper

Sort through the beans, discarding any discolored ones or impurities. Rinse the beans, drain and place in a large saucepan with hot tap water to cover by 3 inches (7.5 cm). Bring to a boil over medium-high heat. Immediately remove from the heat, cover and let stand for 1 hour. ❧ Drain the beans, rinse and drain again. Return the beans to the pan and add the 4 cups (32 fl oz/1 l) hot tap water, bay leaf, orange zest strips stuck with cloves, and the parsley sprigs. Bring to a boil over medium-high heat, reduce the heat to medium-low or low, cover and simmer until the beans are just tender, 1–1½ hours. During the last 15 minutes of cooking, add the salt and season to taste with pepper. ❧ When the beans are done, taste and adjust the seasoning. Remove the bay leaf, orange peel and parsley and discard. Set aside to cool. ❧ The beans can be tightly covered and stored in the refrigerator for 2–3 days. Use any leftover beans in salads, soups or vegetable side dishes.

Makes about 5 cups (2¼ lb/1.1 kg) drained beans; serves 4–6

Green Sauce

2 cloves garlic, minced
¼ cup minced fresh flat-leaf (Italian) parsley
1 tablespoon minced fresh sage
2 tablespoons balsamic vinegar
½ cup (4 fl oz/125 ml) extra-virgin olive oil
Salt

In a small saucepan, combine the garlic, parsley, sage, balsamic vinegar and olive oil. Stir to blend. Place over low heat and warm, stirring, until heated to serving temperature. Season with a little salt, if desired. ❧ Use immediately or set aside and cover to keep warm until needed.

Makes ¾ cup (6 fl oz/180 ml)

Ravioli Dough

2 cups (10 oz/315 g) unbleached all-purpose (plain) flour
1 teaspoon salt
2 tablespoons unsalted butter, cut into small pieces
About ½ cup (4 fl oz/125 ml) boiling water

In a food processor fitted with the metal blade, place the flour and salt. Add the butter and, using on-off pulses, process until granular. Continuing to pulse, slowly add the boiling water until a dough just forms; not all of the water may be needed. (Alternatively, mix the dough by hand in a bowl.) ❧ Gather the dough into a ball and place on a floured work surface. Knead a few times until soft and smooth. Flatten into a rectangle, divide in half and wrap one-half in plastic wrap. ❧ On a well-floured surface, roll out the remaining half into a very thin rectangle about 12 by 16 inches (30 by 40 cm). Cut the rectangle in half crosswise to form 2 rectangles. Lay them on a kitchen towel and top with a second towel. Repeat with the reserved dough.

Makes enough dough for 48–64 round ravioli, each 1½ inches (4 cm) in diameter

To fill ravioli: Using a teaspoon, place small mounds of filling in rows on 1 rectangle, spacing ½ inch (12 mm) apart and ¼ inch (6 mm) in from the sides. Lay a second rectangle on top. Using a round cutter 1½ inches (4 cm) in diameter, cut out each mound. (Or cut into squares with a rolling cutter.) ❧ Press the edges together firmly; place in a single layer on a baking sheet. Cover with a clean towel. Repeat with remaining 2 rectangles.

Hazelnut Meringues

1¼ cups (6½ oz/200 g) hazelnuts (filberts)
¾ cup (6 oz/185 g) superfine (castor) sugar
½ teaspoon cream of tartar
Pinch of salt
¼ teaspoon ground cinnamon
⅛ teaspoon ground ginger
4 egg whites
1 teaspoon vanilla extract (essence)

Position a rack in the middle of an oven and preheat to 325°F (165°C). Spread the hazelnuts on a baking sheet and bake until the nuts begin to change color, are fragrant and the skins split and loosen, 5–10 minutes. Let cool for a few minutes, then wrap the nuts in a clean kitchen towel and rub against them with the palms of your hands to remove most of the skins. Place the nuts in a coarse-mesh sieve and shake the nuts to separate them from their skins. Do not worry if bits of the skins remain. Chop the nuts coarsely and set aside. ❧ Reduce the oven temperature to 275°F (135°C). Cover 2 baking sheets with aluminum foil or parchment (baking) paper. Set aside. ❧ In a small bowl, sift together the superfine sugar, cream of tartar, salt, cinnamon and ginger. Set aside. In a large bowl, combine the egg whites and vanilla. Using a balloon whisk or an electric mixer set on medium speed, whisk or beat until soft folds form. While continuing to beat, add the sugar mixture, a little at a time, beating until stiff, glossy peaks form that hold their shape, 3–4 minutes. Using a rubber spatula, fold in ¾ cup (4 oz/125 g) of the chopped hazelnuts. ❧ Using a teaspoon, form small mounds of the meringue, each ¾–1 inch (2–2.5 cm) in diameter, on the 2 prepared baking sheets, spacing them about ½ inch (12 mm) apart. Sprinkle a few of the remaining nuts on top of each meringue. ❧ Bake until lightly colored, 25–30 minutes. Turn off the oven and prop open the oven door about 1 inch (2.5 cm). Let cool completely, about 2 hours.

Makes 60–70 meringues

Crostini

½ crusty French baguette or Italian country-style bread, 2 inches (5 cm) in diameter and 10–12 inches (25–30 cm) long
Extra-virgin olive oil

Position a rack in the upper part of an oven and preheat to 450°F (230°C). ❧ Using a sharp knife or a serrated bread knife, cut the bread on the diagonal into slices ½ inch (12 mm) thick. Brush each side lightly with olive oil and place on a baking sheet. Bake, turning once, until lightly golden, about 2 minutes on each side. Watch carefully and do not allow the crostini to toast until they are hard. ❧ Serve warm. The crostini can be sprinkled with chopped herbs (fresh or dried) or rubbed with a garlic clove. Or top them with such savory spreads as anchovy, black or green olive, artichoke, or ricotta with herbs.

Makes 24–30 slices

KITCHEN EQUIPMENT

A selection of cookware and tools used in the preparation of the recipes in this collection.

COOKWARE & BAKEWARE

Sturdy pots and pans for stove top and oven.

1. Sauté Pan
For quick searing or browning or for gentle sautéing, stewing or braising, select a well-made heavy metal pan large enough to hold food in a single layer without crowding. Straight sides help retain heat and contain splattering.

2. Frying Pan
Choose good-quality heavy aluminum, stainless steel, cast iron or enameled steel for rapid frying or browning. Shallow, flared sides promote evaporation of moisture.

3. Saucepan
A versatile pan, available in several sizes, for cooking many foods. Select pans made of heavy anodized aluminum, cast aluminum, stainless steel or enameled steel.

4. Double Boiler
A large saucepan topped with a heatproof bowl is excellent for gently warming or melting heat-sensitive foods.

5. Round Cake Pan
Standard-sized pan, 8 or 9 inches (20 or 23 cm) in diameter and 2 inches (5 cm) deep, in aluminum, stainless steel or tinned steel.

6. Springform Pan
Deep, circular pan with spring-clip sides that loosen for easy removal of hard-to-unmold cakes.

7. Baking Pans
Heavy, durable, shallow metal sheet pans for a wide variety of uses, from roasting peppers to toasting nuts to baking breads.

8. Pasta Pot
Large stainless-steel pot includes pierced insert for easy draining.

9. Stove-Top Grill
Sturdy grilling surface of cast aluminum for stove-top grilling of vegetables or other foods.

10. Baking Dishes
Select heavy-duty glazed porcelain, stoneware, earthenware, glass or tinned copper for oven baking.

PREP TOOLS

To help speed along food preparation.

11. Colander
For draining pasta, beans and other foods.

12. Food Processor
For chopping, shredding, grating or slicing large quantities of ingredients with great efficiency and speed. Also useful for making fresh pasta dough.

13. Food Mill
Hand-cranked mill purées cooked potatoes and other ingredients by forcing them through its conical grinding disk, which also strains out fibers, skins and seeds.

14. Mortar and Pestle
For crushing whole spices such as aniseeds to flavor biscotti.

15. Pepper Mill
For freshly grinding peppercorns.

16. Ricer
Sturdy, hinged stainless-steel apparatus forces boiled potatoes through small holes, producing smooth, fine-textured mashed potatoes and purées.

17. Kitchen String
For trussing poultry and tying up bouquets garnis. Select linen string that will withstand intense heat with minimal charring.

18. Parchment Paper
Stick-resistant ovenproof paper for lining baking sheets for delicate meringues and for enclosing oven-baked fish.

UTENSILS

Hand-held tools for general and specific tasks.

19. Skimmer
Wide disk with fine mesh for efficient removal of froth from simmered recipes, and for removing small pieces of food from simmering liquid.

20. Kitchen Knives
Large chef's knife for chopping; thin-bladed, flexible knife for slicing meat and poultry; paring knife for peeling vegetables, cutting up small ingredients and testing meat and poultry for doneness; long serrated blade for cutting bread and roasted meat; two-pronged fork for steadying food during carving.

21. Parmesan Knife
Traditional Italian knife for cutting chunks of Parmesan or other hard cheeses.

22. Basting Brush
For all-purpose brushing of thin, even coatings of oil, lemon juice and other liquid ingredients.

23. Ravioli Cutter
Rolling cutter with decorative serrated edge for cutting ravioli dough.

24. Instant-Read Thermometer
Insert into the thickest part of roasted meat or poultry at the earliest moment it might be done for a quick and accurate measure of internal temperature.

25. Mushroom Brush
Small brush with short, soft bristles for cleaning the delicate surface of mushrooms.

26. Asparagus Peeler
Small, tonglike stainless-steel device grasps and strips away the tough, thin layer of peel from thick asparagus stalks.

27. Hand-Held Grater
Fine rasp surface for grating citrus zest or whole nutmeg.

28. Zester
Small, sharp holes at end of stainless-steel blade cut citrus zest into fine shreds.

29. Fine-Holed Shredder
Hand-held utensil perforated with sharp slots for cutting thin shreds of citrus zest or other ingredients.

30. Meat Pounder
Heavy stainless-steel disk with sturdy handle, to flatten meat or poultry for quick sautéing.

31. Olive Pitter
Small, sturdy device grips an olive and pushes out its pit in one squeeze.

32. Round Cutter
Stainless-steel biscuit or cookie cutter for cutting sheets of fresh pasta dough into round ravioli, or for cutting polenta and semolina gnocchi into rounds.

33. Parmesan Cheese Grater
Half-cylindrical utensil with coarse rasp surface for quickly grating blocks of Parmesan cheese.

34. Box Grater/Shredder
Sturdy stainless-steel tool for grating or shredding ingredients.

35. Assorted Utensils
Basket holds rolling pin for rolling out doughs and for flattening chicken breasts; wooden spoons for all-purpose mixing and stirring; spatulas for turning foods during cooking; metal tongs for picking up or turning ingredients; slotted spoon for transferring cooked meats or vegetables without their liquid; ladle for serving soups and stews; potato masher for mashing potatoes by hand; mesh sieves for draining and straining; and wooden pasta serving forks.

SUGGESTED MENUS

*T*here are no strict rules for composing an Italian menu. An *antipasto* may be served with a pasta and salad for a casual lunch or supper; or two or three *antipasti* served together can comprise a meal on their own. For an informal three-course dinner menu, start with a pasta, soup or salad; follow it with a second course of chicken, fish or meat and a side dish, and then cap off the meal with a light dessert. Just pick and choose from among the many varied courses represented by the chapters in this book, forming menus as free-form or structured, light or hearty as you wish. Here are some suggestions to get you started.

Weekend Brunches or Light Suppers

Assorted Antipasti, page 6
Farfalle with Tuna and Black Olives, page 36
Mixed Berries with Zabaglione, page 117

❧

Shrimp-Filled Artichokes with Mustard Dressing, page 11
Lentil, Tomato and Mint Soup, page 24
Arugula Salad with Black Olive Crostini, page 35
Apple Walnut Cake, page 106

❧

Shrimp and Scallops with Mixed Herbs
and Baby Greens, page 19
Swiss Chard and Poached Eggs with Polenta, page 88
Grape Focaccia, page 100

❧

Baked Semolina Gnocchi, page 39
Escarole Salad with Pear and Prosciutto, page 30
Lemon Rice Pudding with Hazelnut Meringues, page 112

Casual Dinners

Blood Orange, Fennel and Olive Salad, page 32
Baked Salmon on Chard, page 72
Italian Green Beans with Mint, page 86
Lemon Rice Pudding with Hazelnut Meringues, page 112

❧

Green Beans and Tuna with Basil, page 16
Braised Pork Loin with Sage, page 64
Mashed Potatoes with Rosemary and Lemon, page 95
Glazed Carrots with Marsala and Hazelnuts, page 84
Oranges with Mint and Toasted Almonds, page 109

❧

Asparagus with Capers and Pine Nuts, page 15
Sautéed Chicken Breasts with Parmesan Cheese, page 52
Roasted Red Peppers with Oregano, page 92
Pink Grapefruit Granita, page 114
Almond Biscotti, page 110

❧

Cheese and Basil Ravioli, page 40
Fresh Tuna with Mint and Coriander, page 80
Braised Fennel in Milk, page 91
Mixed Berries with Zabaglione, page 117

Serve the Walnut Ring Loaf, Grape Focaccia or Polenta Bread with any of the menus listed here.

ITALIAN INGREDIENTS

An illustrated primer of eight distinctive Italian ingredients, all available in Italian delicatessens and well-stocked food stores.

CANNELLINI BEANS

These small to medium-sized, white, thin-skinned oval beans are among the most popular in Italy, appearing in soups, salads, appetizers, stews and vegetable side dishes. If cannellini cannot be found, Great Northern or white (navy) beans may be substituted. Canned cooked cannellini beans may also be used in some recipes; they should be drained and well rinsed before use.

ARBORIO RICE

A specialty of Italy's Piedmont and Lombardy regions, Arborio rice has short, round grains that cook to a pleasantly chewy texture while developing their own creamy sauce—the distinctive characteristics of risotto. Similar varieties include Vialone Nano and Carnaroli, which is considered the best. Medium-grain white rice can be substituted if Arborio is unavailable.

POLENTA

The term *polenta* refers both to Italian yellow or white cornmeal and to the cooked mush made from it and served as a first course or side dish. In Italy, the best polenta is made from cornmeal freshly ground within the two- to three-week harvest period. I find that long-cooking polenta imported from Italy, with its fine, even grind, has a better flavor and cooks to a smoother and more even consistency than American cornmeal or quick-cooking varieties.

MARSALA

A specialty of the region of Marsala, in Sicily, this aromatic amber wine, which is available in both dry and sweet versions, finds widespread use as a flavoring in the Italian kitchen. It is most often used as the base of a sauce for chicken or veal, for adding color and flavor to carrots, and for enhancing a wide variety of cakes and desserts.

OLIVES

Ripe black olives may be cured in various combinations of salt, seasonings, brines, oils and vinegars. European olives generally offer the most superior flavor and texture. If you can't find such Italian black olives as Gaeta, substitute similar Spanish, Greek Kalamata or French Niçoise olives. If the olives are too salty for your taste, drain and rinse well with cold running water, or soak them in cold water to cover for 30 minutes or more. To pit olives, use an olive pitter (see page 121), which grips the olive while pushing out its pit. Or use a small, sharp knife to carefully slit the olive lengthwise down to the pit, then pry away the flesh.

PARMESAN CHEESE

Sharp, salty and richly flavorful, this hard-crusted cow's milk cheese is aged for up to two years. When grated or shredded, it enriches stuffings and sauces, and is used as a garnish for pastas and other savory dishes. The name of the cheese refers to the city of Parma, in central Italy, but the cheese actually was first developed in an area midway between Parma and the town of Reggio. For the best flavor and texture, buy Parmesan imported from Italy in block form—to grate, shred or shave fresh as needed. Parmesan cheese bearing the official Italian mark "Parmigiano-Reggiano" is considered the best quality of all.

OLIVE OIL

One of the greatest sources of character in Italian cooking, olive oil contributes its fruity flavor to a wide range of savory dishes. Extra-virgin olive oil, the most flavorful of all, is extracted from the fruit on the first pressing, without the use of heat or chemicals; it is used most often in dressings and as a seasoning. Each brand sold displays its own distinctive taste and color; higher-priced labels usually offer the best quality. Pure olive oil, which is less aromatic and flavorful, is used most often in cooking. Store all olive oils in airtight containers away from heat and light.

ITALIAN BREAD

Everyday Italian meals are most often accompanied by crusty country-style bread made from unbleached wheat flour and noted for its firm, coarse-textured crumb. Look for round, oval and long loaves in good bakeries and Italian delicatessens, variously labeled Italian, country-style, rustic or peasant bread.

TECHNIQUES

The following pages illustrate practical cooking techniques used in this book that may not be familiar to some readers.

KNEADING DOUGH

Today, more and more people are making bread with the help of food processors and automatic bread machines. But those who make use of such modern conveniences are missing out on the simple, satisfying pleasure of kneading dough by hand. Kneading develops the texture of bread, knitting its gluten into a tight, elastic network that traps the gas emitted by yeast; and there is no better way to tell when a dough has been properly kneaded than by the human touch. That's not to say you can't take some shortcuts: Try the new strains of quick-rise yeast, widely available in stores today, which can significantly reduce the rising time of bread dough. 🦪

PEELING & SEEDING TOMATOES

Tomatoes are one of the great pleasures of the table—especially at the height of summer, when you should seek out the best sun-ripened tomatoes you can find. At other times of year, plum tomatoes, sometimes called Roma or egg tomatoes, are likely to have the best flavor and texture. Often when tomatoes are made into sauces or combined with other ingredients, recipes call for removing their skins and seeds, neither of which contributes much to the prized flavor or texture of the vegetable-fruit. 🦪

1. LOOSENING THE SKIN.
Cut out the core from the stem end of each tomato. Then cut a shallow X in the skin at the tomato's base. Submerge the tomatoes in boiling water for 20–30 seconds. Using a slotted spoon, remove each tomato and submerge in a bowl of cold water.

1. FOLDING OVER THE DOUGH.
Mix the dough as directed in the recipe and turn it out onto a well-floured work surface. Using the heel of your hand, press the dough down and away from you. Then fold the dough over onto itself. Rotate the dough slightly.

2. PEELING THE TOMATO.
Starting at the X, peel the skin from each tomato, using your fingertips and, if necessary, the knife blade.

2. CONTINUING TO KNEAD.
Once more, press down with the heel of your hand, fold the dough over and rotate it. Continue kneading in this manner, working in more flour if necessary to reduce stickiness, until soft, smooth and elastic, about 10 minutes.

3. SEEDING THE TOMATO.
Cut each tomato in half crosswise. Holding each half over a bowl, squeeze gently to force out the seed sacs.

DRAINING & SAUCING PASTA

The cooking time for any pasta will vary with its shape, size and degree of dryness. You can use the package instructions as a guide, but start to test the pasta at the earliest time it might be done by pulling out a piece, blowing on it to cool it slightly and then biting into it. In Italy, perfectly cooked pasta is described as *al dente*—literally, "to the tooth"—tender but still chewy. Don't drain the cooked pasta so thoroughly that its surface becomes dry. Italian cooks leave some water on the pasta, making it easier to mix with the sauce before serving.

ROASTING BELL PEPPERS

Bell peppers (capsicums)—especially the ripened red, yellow and orange varieties—have a natural sweetness and a juicy texture that are heightened by roasting. While many different methods exist for roasting peppers, the one shown here streamlines the process by halving, stemming and seeding them first, leaving only the peeling of the blistered skins after the peppers have cooled.

1. COOKING AND DRAINING.
Cook the pasta in ample quantities of boiling salted water until *al dente*—tender but still chewy. Drain immediately.

2. ADDING PASTA TO THE SAUCE.
The moment excess water has drained from the pasta, add the pasta—with water still clinging to its surface—to the hot prepared sauce.

3. MIXING PASTA AND SAUCE TOGETHER.
With wooden spoons, gently mix the sauce into the pasta to coat evenly. If necessary, warm over medium-high heat for a few seconds. Serve at once.

1. HALVING, STEMMING AND SEEDING.
Preheat a broiler (griller) or an oven to 500°F (260°C). Using a small, sharp knife, cut each pepper in half lengthwise. Cut out the stem, seeds and white ribs from each half.

2. ROASTING THE PEPPERS.
Lay the pepper halves, cut sides down, on a baking sheet. Place under the broiler or in the oven. Broil (grill) or roast until the skins blister and begin to blacken.

3. PEELING THE PEPPERS.
Remove from the oven and cover with aluminum foil. Let steam until cool enough to handle, 10–15 minutes. Then, using your fingers or a knife, peel off the skins.

TRIMMING ARTICHOKES

If you grow up eating artichokes, as most Italians do, these thistlelike vegetables seem commonplace. But those of us who first encounter them in adulthood may be a bit intimidated by the idea of preparing them. As with any vegetable, the secret to getting them ready for cooking is to cut away the parts you wouldn't eat anyway: the tough outer leaves and prickly top, the tough stem portion and, in the case of mature artichokes, the fibrous choke. Be sure to keep some lemon juice close at hand to coat the cut surfaces of each artichoke, which otherwise would quickly turn brown. 🐚

1. REMOVING OUTER LEAVES.

Working with 1 artichoke at a time and starting at the wide bottom, remove the tough outer leaves. Pull each leaf straight down and snap it off. Remove 3 or 4 layers until you reach pale green leaves.

2. CUTTING OFF THE STEM.

Using a sharp knife, cut off the stem of the artichoke even with the bottom.

3. TRIMMING THE TOP.

Cut off the top half or more of the artichoke to eliminate the tough portion. For fully grown artichokes, spread open the center and, using a small spoon or melon baller, scoop out the prickly choke from the center and discard.

CUTTING CITRUS ZEST

Zest, the thin, brightly colored, outermost layer of a citrus fruit's peel, contains most of the peel's aromatic essential oils—which provide a lively source of flavor for savory and sweet dishes alike. Depending upon how the zest will be combined with other ingredients, how intense a citrus flavor is desired and what decorative effects are called for, the zest may be removed in one of several different ways, shown below. Whichever way you use, take care to remove the colored zest only; the white, spongy pith beneath is bitter and, if included, can mar the flavor of the dish. 🐚

GRATING ZEST.

For very fine particles of citrus zest, lightly rub the fruit against the small rasps of a hand-held grater, taking care not to grate away any of the bitter white pith beneath the zest.

SHREDDING ZEST.

Using a simple tool known as a zester, draw its sharp-edged holes across the fruit's skin to remove the zest in thin shreds. Alternatively, use a fine-holed shredder, which has small indented slots to cut shreds.

CUTTING WIDE STRIPS.

Holding the edge of a paring knife or vegetable peeler almost parallel to the fruit's skin, carefully cut off the zest in strips, taking care not to remove any white pith with it.

ACKNOWLEDGMENTS

I am indebted to the late Elizabeth David and to Marcella Hazan for their generosity in sharing, over the years, their love of Italian cooking. My gratitude to the late Raneri di San Faustino for showing me how to make, cook and eat pasta, and to Judy Rodgers and Emalee Chapman for their interpretations of the flavors and simplicity of Italian cooking. I am also grateful to the many restaurateurs in whose establishments I have eaten during my yearly trips to Italy. I would like to thank John Owen for developing this three-book series; Wendely Harvey for her publishing wisdom; Laurie Wertz, Norman Kolpas and Sharon Silva for their expert editorial work; Allan Rosenberg and Allen Lott for their faithful photographic interpretations; Sandra Griswold and Heidi Gintner for beautifully styling the photographs; Alice Harth for her excellent illustrations; John Bull for his creative book design; and everyone else who contributed their time and knowledge to the production of this book.

—Chuck Williams

The publishers would like to thank the following people for their generous assistance and support:
Sharon C. Lott, Stephen W. Griswold, Lorraine Puckett, Linda Clare, Angela Williams, Elaine Anderson, Jennifer Hauser, Jennifer Mullins, Stephani Grant, Marguerite Ozburn, Lawrence Azerrad, Mick Bagnato, and Tim Murray of Purcell-Murray Company Inc.

The following kindly lent props for the photography, in San Francisco: Beaver Bros. Antiques, Biordi Art Imports, Elizabeth C. Davis, Fillamento, Sue Fisher King, Pottery Barn (Chestnut St.), Williams-Sonoma (Post St.) and Chuck Williams

INDEX

almonds
   almond biscotti 110
   oranges with mint and toasted almonds 109
antipasti
   asparagus with capers and pine nuts 15
   assorted antipasti 6
   bruschetta trio 8
   grilled vegetables with herbed dressing 12
   and menu planning 122
   roasted red peppers with oregano 92
   shrimp-filled artichokes with mustard dressing 11
   shrimp and scallops with mixed herbs and
      baby greens 19
apple walnut cake 106
Arborio rice. See rice
   description of 123
artichokes
   assorted antipasti 6
   baked chicken with 55
   boiled beef with green sauce 68
   shrimp-filled with mustard dressing 11
   trimming, description of 126
arugula
   arugula salad with black olive crostini 35
   fettuccine with asparagus and 42
asparagus
   asparagus with capers and pine nuts 15
   fettuccine with asparagus and arugula 42

beans. See cannellini beans; green beans
beef, boiled with green sauce 68
berries, mixed, with zabaglione 117
biscotti, almond 110
blood orange, fennel and olive salad 32
bread
   crostini 119
   grape focaccia 100
   Italian bread, description of 123
   kneading dough for, description of 124
   polenta bread 102
   walnut ring loaf 105
broccoli, penne with tomato and 46
bruschetta trio 8
budino 112

cake, apple walnut 106
cannellini beans
   assorted antipasti 6
   basic recipe for 118
   cannellini bean soup 29
   description of 123
   minestrone 23
carrots, glazed with Marsala and hazelnuts 84
chicken
   baked chicken with artichokes 55
   boiled chicken and ham 59
   braised chicken with eggplant and orange 56
   roasted rosemary chicken 50
   sautéed chicken breasts with Parmesan 52

cookies
   hazelnut meringues 119
crab, saffron risotto with 49
crostini
   assorted antipasti 6
   arugula salad with black olive crostini 35
   basic recipe for 119
   polenta crostini 45
   shrimp and scallops with mixed herbs and
      baby greens 19

desserts
   almond biscotti 110
   apple walnut cake 106
   hazelnut meringues 119
   lemon rice pudding with hazelnut meringues 112
   mixed berries with zabaglione 117
   oranges with mint and toasted almonds 109
   pink grapefruit granita 114
dressings
   mustard 11
   herbed 12

eggplant
   braised chicken with eggplant and orange 56
   grilled vegetables with herbed dressing 12
eggs
   Swiss chard and poached eggs with polenta 88
equipment, description of 121
escarole salad with pears and prosciutto 30

farfalle with tuna and black olives 36
fennel
    blood orange, fennel and olive salad 32
    braised fennel in milk 91
    grilled vegetables with herbed dressing 12
    seafood stew 75
fettuccine with asparagus and arugula 42
fish. *See* seafood
focaccia
    basic recipe for 118
    grape focaccia 100

gnocchi, baked semolina 39
granita, pink grapefruit 114
grape focaccia 100
grapefruit granita 114
green beans
    green beans and tuna with basil 16
    Italian green beans with mint 86
green sauce 68, 118

halibut with tomatoes and pine nuts 79
ham, boiled chicken and 59
hazelnut meringues 119

lamb stew with polenta 71
lemon rice pudding with hazelnut meringues 112
lentil, tomato and mint soup 24

Marsala wine
    description of 123
    glazed carrots with Marsala and hazelnuts 84
    saffron risotto with crab 49
    veal scaloppine with Marsala 60
menu planning 122
meringues, hazelnut 112, 119
minestrone 23
mushrooms
    assorted antipasti 6
    sautéed zucchini and 96
mussels
    seafood stew 75

olives, description of 123
orange
    blood orange, fennel and olive salad 32
    braised chicken with eggplant and orange 56
    oranges with mint and toasted almonds 109
osso buco 67

Parmesan cheese, description of 123
pasta
    cheese and basil ravioli 40
    draining and saucing pastas 125
    farfalle with tuna and black olives 36
    fettuccine with asparagus and arugula 42
    penne with tomato and broccoli 46

penne with tomato and broccoli 46
peppers
    baked peppers stuffed with Italian sausage 63
    bruschetta trio 8
    roasted red peppers with oregano 92
    roasting, description of 125
polenta
    description of 123
    fried polenta squares 45
    lamb stew with 71
    polenta bread 102
    polenta crostini 45
    polenta with Parmesan cheese 45
    Swiss chard and poached eggs with 88
pork loin, braised, with sage 64
potatoes, mashed, with rosemary and lemon 95
prosciutto, escarole salad with pears and 30
pudding, lemon rice 112

radicchio
    grilled vegetables with herbed dressing 12
ravioli
    cheese and basil 40
    ravioli dough, recipe for 119
rice
    Aborio, description of 123
    fresh tomato and bread soup with basil 20
    lemon rice pudding 112
    saffron risotto with crab 49
    spinach and rice soup 26
risotto, saffron, with crab 49

saffron risotto with crab 49
salads
    arugula salad with black olive crostini 35
    blood orange, fennel and olive salad 32
    escarole salad with pears and prosciutto 30
salmon, baked on chard 72
sauce, green 68, 118
sausage, baked peppers stuffed with Italian 63
scallops
    shrimp and scallops with mixed herbs and
      baby greens 19
sea bass, baked in parchment 83
seafood
    baked salmon on chard 72
    baked sea bass in parchment 83
    broiled swordfish with green olives 76
    farfalle with tuna and black olives 36
    fresh tuna with mint and coriander 80
    green beans and tuna with basil 16
    halibut with tomatoes and pine nuts 79
    saffron risotto with crab 49
    seafood stew 75
    shrimp and scallops with mixed herbs and
      baby greens 19
    shrimp-filled artichokes with mustard dressing 11

shrimp
    seafood stew 75
    shrimp and scallops with mixed herbs and
      baby greens 19
    shrimp-filled artichokes with mustard dressing 11
soups
    cannellini bean soup 29
    fresh tomato and bread soup with basil 20
    lentil, tomato and mint soup 24
    minestrone 23
    spinach and rice soup 26
spinach
    and rice soup 26
    saffron risotto with crab 49
    shrimp and scallops with mixed herbs and
      baby greens 19
stews
    lamb stew with polenta 71
    seafood stew 75
Swiss chard
    baked salmon on chard 72
    minestrone 23
    Swiss chard and poached eggs with polenta 88
swordfish with green olives, broiled 76

tomatoes, peeling and seeding 124
tuna
    farfalle with tuna and black olives 36
    fresh tuna with mint and coriander 80
    green beans and tuna with basil 16

veal scaloppine with Marsala 60
veal shanks, braised 67
vegetables
    baked peppers stuffed with Italian sausage 63
    baked salmon on chard 72
    baked stuffed tomatoes with basil 99
    braised fennel in milk 91
    cucumber relish 72
    glazed carrots with Marsala and hazelnuts 84
    green beans and tuna with basil 16
    Italian green beans with mint 86
    grilled vegetables with herbed dressing 12
    mashed potatoes with rosemary and lemon 95
    roasted red peppers with oregano 92
    sautéed zucchini and mushrooms 96
    Swiss chard and poached eggs with polenta 88
walnuts
    apple walnut cake 106
    cheese and basil ravioli 40
    walnut ring loaf 105

zabaglione, mixed berries with 117
zest, cutting 126
zucchini
    grilled vegetables with herbed dressing 12
    sautéed zucchini and mushrooms 96